TURN

How the World's Top
AUTO DEALERS
ARE TURNING THINGS AROUND
By Focusing on the Customer,
NOT THE CAR.

Published by CelebrityPress™, Orlando, FL
A division of The Celebrity Branding Agency®

Celebrity Branding® is a registered trademark
Printed in the United States of America.

ISBN: 9780985364328
LCCN: 2012936235

This publication is designed to provide accurate and authoritative information with regard to the subject matter covered. It is sold with the understanding that the publisher is not engaged in rendering legal, accounting, or other professional advice. If legal advice or other expert assistance is required, the services of a competent professional should be sought. The opinions expressed by the authors in this book are not endorsed by CelebrityPress™ and are the sole responsibility of the author rendering the opinion.

Most CelebrityPress™ titles are available at special quantity discounts for bulk purchases for sales promotions, premiums, fundraising, and educational use. Special versions or book excerpts can also be created to fit specific needs.

For more information, please write:

CelebrityPress™
520 N. Orlando Ave, #2
Winter Park, FL 32789
or call 1.877.261.4930

Visit us online at www.CelebrityPressPublishing.com

TURN

How the World's Top

AUTO DEALERS

ARE TURNING THINGS AROUND
By Focusing on the Customer,
NOT THE CAR.

Contents

CHAPTER 14
HERE TO SERVE: NEVER MAKE A CUSTOMER HALF-HAPPY!

Introduction

By Jimmy Vee and Travis Miller

If you've picked up this book you may be wondering why anyone would write a book about car dealers. Or, frankly, why anyone would want to *read* a book about car dealers. We'll get to the second part in just a moment, but first let's tackle who we are and why we would embark on the odd journey of writing a book about innovation in the car business.

We're Jim and Travis, two guys who wrote a best-selling book and started a company that helps people make their businesses and their lives much better by teaching them how to stand out and make themselves special. We're unconventional guys who do things in unconventional ways. In fact, it's our "buck-the-system" approach to life that has allowed us to achieve a high degree of success in business and life in a short amount of time. During our steep and rocky journey to find success we tried many tactics to get attention, make things happen and create prosperity. On that journey, we failed *a lot* … and we learned *a lot* about what it takes to stand out and succeed.

We could go on for days about all the lessons we've learned. That topic alone could fill an encyclopedia. But what we want to share with you in this book is the one lesson that has truly had the greatest impact on us and the many business leaders we have mentored over the years ... and how that simple secret has enormous power to make your life better.

THE MOST *UNOBVIOUS* TRUTH

This simple secret is hiding in plain sight; most of us miss it everyday. What was once invisible to us is now one of our guiding principles and our most coveted secret to success. The concept is simple, but it's not easy to implement. The reason most people don't "get it" is because of the mental shift required to truly embrace the idea. If you think you're ready, here it is: "SAME IS LAME."

If you look up the word "lame" over at http://www.vocabulary. com it is defined as, "Pathetically lacking in force and effectiveness." We can all agree that if you lack force and effectiveness in life you won't get very far. But if same *is* lame, then when you act and make choices like everyone else, you will, by definition, lack force and effectiveness. But aren't force and effectiveness necessary tools to stand out and succeed in life?

Remember, consensus doesn't make right. Just because "everyone" is doing it one way doesn't make it the best way. Frequently, the best solution to a problem is the one people are least likely to choose. The solutions that are the most unique are often the most unpopular on the surface. The ideas that are the most unpopular and least likely to be chosen are also the ones that are most interesting to people because they are extraordinary. In many cases, the best choice is the least common choice. Unconventional and different ideas get noticed and get talked about. Business strategist Seth Godin said it best when he wrote, "Safe is the riskiest place you can be," in his best-selling book *Purple Cow.*

OUR MISSION TO FIND UNCOMMON GREATNESS

One of our missions in life is to reveal this secret to as many people as possible. We're always on the hunt for ways our ideas can have the greatest impact. We believe life and business should be ESP—Enjoyable, Simple & Prosperous. The secret of "Same Is Lame" and the results that come from being unique and doing things differently is a quick way to create ESP in your life and business. One question we continually ask others and ourselves is, "Who can benefit most from this message?" One of the answers that came up repeatedly in our discussions was ... car dealers.

The car business is an industry of sameness—of lameness. It is an industry plagued by people who do and act the same way everyone else around them acts. It's industry where local dealers are prompted by the upper echelon to be the same, ordinary and average.

It's an industry being pushed into commoditization and homogenization, supposedly for its own good. Our view is that commoditization and homogenization is not good for any industry, or anyone for that matter. Individualization and uniqueness breed innovation, and innovations solve problems for people.

We decided recently that taking our message to car dealers could be a huge opportunity for creating change on a massive scale and felt the car business was the perfect place for us to make a major difference in the world. We knew some dealers would embrace our secret, and we knew there must be some dealers out there who were already working against the machine and flourishing by going against the grain and doing things differently. We made it our mission to find them and foster their desire to stand out, lead the charge of change and be an example others could follow.

So, we set out on a mission to find the most special car dealers in existence. Those unique dealers who broke the rules and busted out of the stereotype. We sought out dealers who didn't have just customers, but had actual FANS! We wanted to find car dealers who earned the loyalty of their customers and kept their customers for generations. We looked for dealers who were achieving celebrity status in their hometowns, dealers who gave back to their communities, dealers who were making the world a better place, dealers who deserve respect and admiration, dealers who believe there is more to selling cars than advertising fake low prices.

And, boy, did we ever find them! We've sifted through the emotional stories of thousands of car-buying customers and uncovered a handful of true gems in the car business. Dealers where we would send our mothers to buy a car. Now, here in your hands, you're holding a directory of the best car dealers in America. If you're lucky enough to have one of these dealers in your town, you should count your blessings. If not, you should consider traveling to do business with one of these rare dealers.

We discovered that these men and women who are unconventional examples of excellence and innovation in a worn-out, old business are good people just like you and us. They have families; they have good days and bad days; they have faith; they have worries; they have hopes and dreams. And most of all, they have a burning desire to think different, to act different and to truly be different.

It's our pleasure to present to you the finest car dealers in America. These dealers are on a mission to turn around the car business, one customer at a time.

CHAPTER 1

Returning to Roots Puts Dealership on Successful Path for the Future

By Torrey Blackwell

I feel that I must give you a little history about our family and our business in order for you to understand why I had to make a U-Turn!

I'm a third-generation new-car dealer in Danville, Va., and my family has been in the car business for more than 70 years. My grandfather, Tony Blackwell, started out as a mechanic at the local Buick store. After working there for 14 years, he decided to open his own repair shop and Blackwell Auto Repair was born in 1940. Because of my grandfather's reputation as a skilled, honest mechanic, customers began bringing their Buicks to his shop for their service needs.

In addition to servicing cars, Tony would repair and sell used cars as well. People enjoyed buying a car from a mechanic they knew and trusted. Blackwell Motor Co. was formed in 1941 and grew faster than expected because of my grandfather's reputation as one of the area's best mechanics. My father, Tom Blackwell, grew up turning wrenches with his father, and he also became a fine mechanic over the years. The father-and-son team would work side by side late into the night finishing work on their customers' cars. From mechanical repairs to body work and painting, Blackwell Motor Co serviced all makes and models.

Ferguson Tractor, Austin-Healey, Hudson, Rambler, and American Motors were the brands that my grandfather represented during his first 20 years as a dealer. In 1967, the Dodge franchise was purchased, and the Blackwells moved into a new dealership. In those days, cars that weren't GM or Ford products were considered "off-brand" cars; always selling the off-brand, new cars meant that Blackwell Motor Co. had to appeal to the consumer in different ways. It was not always price, but the way that the Blackwells took care of their customers like family that made the difference. My grandfather and father would trade for anything to help someone get into a nicer, newer car—guns, land, houses, livestock, tractors, lawn mowers, watches and more were commonly accepted trades in those days.

Blackwell's advertising was seen as controversial by other dealers in Danville. Full-page newspaper ads with lots of pictures and radio events touting the theme of the month kept the local dealers wondering what Tony and Tom would do next. A father and son running a dealership by gut instinct while treating people like family was proving to be successful. My father eventually bought the dealership and expanded into three stores representing several new-car franchises such as Chrysler, Plymouth, Jeep, Eagle, GMC Trucks, Lincoln Mercury, Fiat, Toyota and Kia.

I consider my father as the maverick of the car business in our Danville market. He was never afraid of a challenge and, in the Blackwell entrepreneurial way, always looking for the next opportunity. In the early 70s, when he expanded into a market 30 miles away with a new dealership, the manufacturers were still frowning on the idea of one dealer owning multiple franchises in several markets. In the decades to come, the manufacturer mentality would reverse itself and agree that my father's model was a good one.

My father, now 83 years old, still visits the dealership weekly—arriving in his Dodge Magnum. He enjoys striking up conversations with customers in the lounge and making sure that they are satisfied. A devout Christian, my father keeps a basket of miniature scripture books in the lounge for customers to pick up if they wish. He is constantly refilling this basket with miniature Bibles. His entrepreneurial spirit along with his faith have guided this business and made him into one of the area's most reputable dealers.

TORREY'S EARLY DAYS

My pretend dealership from childhood was made up of a Matchbox and Hot Wheels collection. Cars, trucks, jeeps, vans and a miniature service department complete with a gas station made up my pretend Blackwell Dodge. I would wash my tricycle and pretend to gas it up like I worked in the detail department and then arrange my lot for a big sale. I knew exactly what I wanted to do when I grew up: be the boss at my Dad's dealership!

Childhood dreams became a reality. I graduated from the University of Richmond in 1989; after working at the Virginia Automobile Dealers Association, I decided it was time to head home and get into the family business. My fiancee and I moved back home and got married; and I dove head first into the dealership.

But transitions like this are never smooth. Employees were often resentful of the boss' son being at the store. I had lots of ideas and wanted to change things for the better. I had attended finance and insurance school in Dearborn, Mich., and came back ready to set the woods on fire. I still remember a classmate talking about sending credit applications to banks over a facsimile machine. When I returned from school I was ready to add this awesome new technology to our store. I still remember the sales manager saying that he did not understand why we needed a fax machine. He continued to argue that we could just pick up the phone and call the bank. I still don't understand why people always fight change!

After successfully running several of our dealerships since 1990, in 2006, I built an impressive 38,000 square-foot dealership for Chrysler, Jeep, Dodge and Kia franchises in Danville. In the beginning, business was good, but soon the price of gas went through the roof and the financial crisis of 2009 brought everything to a halt. Business was bad. I now had huge overhead with a new building, and Chrysler was filing for bankruptcy. I still remember my Chrysler sales representative calling me to say that no one was safe in this bankruptcy. However, when the list of surviving dealers came out we made the cut. I was relieved but also sad as I watched several of my dealer friends lose everything overnight.

Soon Chrysler Financial made their dealer body aware that they were no longer going to provide lines of credit for inventory. Luckily, GMAC/Ally announced an interim floor plan for Chrysler dealers to keep them in business. I was relieved, but this interim line of credit was not sufficient to operate, and it took more cash than ever to keep the business running. But because the financial markets were in such a mess and Chrysler's bankruptcy, GMAC/Ally was our only source.

I was getting angrier by the minute. Business was tough enough without the banks pulling the rug out from under us. After months of negotiations, our interim floor plan was made permanent, and I vowed at that moment that something had to change. The Great Recession had made it almost impossible for me to stay in business; in order to survive another downturn I needed to make some major changes.

U-TURN

The culture of our store needed a makeover, but in reality, I was the one who needed the biggest makeover. The Chrysler bankruptcy had taken its toll on my attitude. My father has always believed that when life gets tough you put everything in the Lord's hands, pray about your situation, work harder, cut expenses and you will survive. But I was working myself to death, and it was taking its toll. So, I began reading books about successful business owners, biographies of leaders, self-help books, books on spirituality and the Bible. These sources of inspiration rekindled my own spirit along with my faith, and I was determined to change the atmosphere and attitude at Blackwell Automotive.

Over the years, the automobile manufacturers had succeeded in making our buildings look the same, our promotions look the same, and my dealership into a cookie-cutter, factory store. We had the look, but over the years Blackwell had lost its identity.

Looking back through our history, I could see that my father and grandfather had taken extreme risk and never conformed to the marketing of the masses. They stood out as different kinds of dealers. The owners were mechanics with high school educations who could relate easily to their clients. Back in the day, Blackwell Motor Co. would go to extreme measures to make a deal. I remember as a child my dad trading for pigs, guns, land, boats and trailers. Where had that spirit gone? I had failed to keep that philosophy to the degree that my father and grandfather had.

Don't get me wrong here, I always maintained the company integrity and treated people with honor and respect, but somewhere over the years I fell into the trap of following what the manufacturers and other dealers were doing. That conformity had killed my spirit and the identity of the store as well. I was determined to take our dealership back to its roots and to have fun again in the car business!

I would not go through another recession without the ability to survive. The parts and service division got an overhaul—including some much needed personnel and process changes to better satisfy our customers. I met with all the employees and told them what was expected and let them know if they didn't change then they would need to find a job elsewhere. I'm sorry to say that we had some employee turnover, but in every case, the new employees outperformed their old counterparts. To my delight, attitudes in every department began to change. The negativity that stemmed from Chrysler's bankruptcy receded, and the departments began to flourish. The new employees were all thankful for their jobs and appreciated working at Blackwell Automotive. The service and parts division now had new personnel and new processes along with some great long-term employees who had always maintained the right attitude. We had only just begun.

The sales department needed an adjustment as well. The Chrysler bankruptcy and the loss of stores by my friends made me aware of just how close I had come to losing my dealership. I could have been that credit-challenged father walking into a dealership needing someone to help me find transportation. I vowed that everyone, regardless of their credit score, would be treated like family when they entered our store and that we would try everything in our power to get them approved for a nicer, newer car. I established relationships with several new banks to help our credit-challenged customers get the car they deserved. Our new mantra became "The Dealer For The People®" because I wanted everyone to be treated equally no matter what their credit situation. To facilitate this further, I changed my sales team to a noncommissioned pay plan. Our noncommissioned salespeople treat everyone like family, and they specialize in finding solutions to our customers' transportation problems. My store is known as the "no fear zone" because our customers will not be pressured by our sales professionals.

I started marketing our newfound culture using monthly promotions with myself as the spokesperson for Blackwell Chrysler Jeep Dodge Kia. I was proud to return to the roots of our dealership with campaigns stating that we would trade for anything— just like my father had done years earlier. I've traded for gold, silver, coins, four wheelers, Harleys, boats, tractors, Gators, trailers, Wii game systems and even a tanning bed in order to make a deal happen!

I'm extremely proud of my noncommissioned sales staff members who take pride in taking care of our customers just like family. And my credit approval gurus will do everything in their power to get our customers approved. We will also go to the extreme to locate the car of your dreams! If we don't have what you're looking for, we'll find it, guaranteed!

My service and parts staff will service any make or model just like my father and grandfather did for decades. We stock parts for all makes as well, and our Express Lane is open for fast oil changes and more. If you're in the market for a nicer, newer car give us a call or visit us 24/7 at www.blackwellautos.com.

TIPS FOR CAR SHOPPERS

Here are some questions to ask and some insider information to be aware of the next time you go car shopping.

1. **How long has the dealer been in business?**
   Longevity says a lot about the dealer's commitment to the community and its customers. A business that has been around for decades means that the dealer has been around during good times and bad and that they will more than likely always be there to serve you. Some dealers show up as the new kid on the block and then in three to five years the store is sold, another person is running the dealership, or it goes out of business. Look for a store that has been around for a while under the same ownership with a good reputation. These dealers are the ones that you know, like and trust! They will be there for service after the sale, and they will gladly administer any service contract, gap, credit life and accident and health insurance claims.

2. **Does the name on the building represent the owner or a minority partner thrown into the store to run it for a large dealer group?**
   With the growth of mega-dealer groups, more and more dealerships are owned by large dealers who place a minority owner in the community to run the dealership.

Even the advertising and the dealership make the community think that the minority partner owns the whole enchilada! Do your research and know who you are dealing with and who is the majority owner of the dealership. In most cases, minority owners can be moved out quickly and another partner moved in over night.

3. Do the warranties and maintenance plans sound too good to be true?

Lifetime warranties??? I can't believe that people fall for these every day! I have customers bringing in cars to my service department every day wanting to know if their lifetime warranty is still valid since the XYZ dealer they bought the car from went out of business. And in case after case, we have to tell them that we are sorry, but that lifetime warranty was good only at the store you purchased it from. These warranties have lots of loopholes built in to make it advantageous for the dealer and the insurance company—not the consumer. Usually all required services must be performed at the dealership and if you miss just one by a few miles then your claim can be rejected. Remember—if it sounds too good to be true then it probably is!

4. Is the owner available and working at the store, or is he or she an absentee dealer?

Many dealers are not available, and they rarely even come into the store. Ask your sales professional if you can meet or talk with the owner. This step is important because if issues arise down the road with your automobile or warranty then you want to know that the owner is there to handle the situation.

5. Take a tour of the service and parts department before you agree to buy your next car.

This is one of the most important aspects of a dealership. You should ask to meet the service and parts mangers before you buy your next car. The departments should be clean, and the technicians should be trained and certified to work on your new car. Surprisingly, some dealers actually neglect the training of their service and parts personnel. Does the service division offer convenient hours, shuttle service, express lane service and a nice customer lounge? You should be impressed by the managers and their departments!

6. What is the atmosphere of the store?

Do you like the feel of the dealership when you enter the building? Is it clean, and is the staff friendly and helpful? Are you offered popcorn, a bottle of water or a soda? In my opinion, you should feel like you just entered a friend's house when you walk into a dealership. That first impression should tell you a lot about the dealership and the owner's commitment to the customer.

7. How are the salespeople paid? Do they work on commission?

The majority of salespeople are paid a commission based on the gross profit of the transaction. That pay system means it a salesperson's goal to get you to pay the MOST possible for the car of your dreams. Non-commissioned sales professionals are paid a salary and then a bonus when a car is sold. Their compensation is not related to the profit on your purchase; therefore, they can spend time finding solutions to your automotive problems instead of pushing a product on you that you don't want. A noncommissioned sales team shows the dealers' commitment to the consumer!

8. Will the store trade for anything?

Many stores will refuse to trade for anything that is not an automobile, and that practice really shows a lack of commitment to the customer. Think about it! If a dealer is trying to help you buy your dream car, then the dealer should at least be willing to look at anything that you have to trade. Sometimes customers need an additional down payment as required by the lender but they never think about the stuff in the garage that they could sell. A dealer who wants your business should always be willing to look at any items that you have for trade!

THE BLESSINGS OF ROOTS

Returning to the roots of Blackwell Motor Co. and bringing our store back to the basics would not have been possible without our wonderful team of employees and our customers. Our business has been blessed with many customers who have become our friends and members of the Blackwell Automotive Family. I'm honored and humbled to still sit with customers every month who bought cars from my father and grandfather!

Constant change and improvement is now a part of our dealership's culture. Some of our ideas that we implement are failures and others are successful, but I believe that failure to implement can cause the demise of any organization. New processes and ideas as well as returning to our roots has brought about much chaos, but I now love working to constantly improve and change my store so that we can thrive for the next 70 years!

And I thank God every day for helping me find "FUN" once again in the car business!

About Torrey

Torrey Blackwell, owner of Blackwell Chrysler Jeep Dodge Kia in Dazzling Danville, Va., has been married to his high school sweetheart, Shelley Blackwell, for 21 years. They have three children, Key, 15; Noah, 13; and Lucy, 8. In Torrey's spare time, he enjoys hanging out at his farm or at the lake with his wife and children. Customers and employees are surprised when he pulls up in an old truck, dressed in camouflage after hunting with his boys. Recently, he has been known to walk through the showroom in his overalls to hand off a dozen fresh eggs from Lucy's chickens.

Torrey is an author and consumer advocate who believes that everyone deserves a nicer, newer car no matter what their credit situation. He is frequently seen on local TV, touting his latest monthly promotion and sometimes taking it to the extreme by wearing pickle costumes and Uncle Sam suits.

Known as "The Dealer For The People,®" he is proud of his noncommissioned sales force and how they help customers find solutions to their automotive problems. He has instilled this philosophy in his parts and service departments as well. Just like his father and grandfather, Blackwell Chrysler Jeep Dodge Kia services all makes and models; and with its Express Lane service an appointment is never needed for an oil change! Remember that Torrey will trade for anything to make a car deal!

Torrey can be reached at 434-792-8853 or online at www.blackwellautos.com.

CHAPTER 2

A True Entrepreneur: From Diners to Drivers

By Scott McCormick

Talk about going from zero to 80 in no time flat. Well, that's just what I did in the car business. In 2008, with absolutely no experience in selling cars, I launched Wausau Auto and Antigo Auto, with a dogged perseverance and a business strategy that has proven to be recession- proof. Even though the bulk of my experience had been in the restaurant industry, I went from selling zero to 80 cars a month and acquired a lifetime's worth of knowledge about the auto industry in the less than 40 months I've been involved in it.

I'd like to share with you certain lessons about how to be open to opportunities outside your comfort zone and how your current business knowledge can set you up for success. You may be surprised at how far these lessons might take you—no matter what you do for a living.

ACCIDENTALLY IN THE AUTO BIZ

In this book you'll hear from other great dealers who became involved in selling cars because they are second- or third-generation dealers or because they have some other long-term connection or experience in the auto industry. In my case, selling cars really never crossed my mind before I ended up actually doing it.

I got involved in the car business by accident while pursuing the development of a restaurant location. For a variety of reasons, the restaurant deal fell through, but I most definitely did not want to lose the A+ real estate location in Wausau, Wis. My challenge became how to keep the location and also find a way to make it stand on its own and generate the necessary revenue to cover my carrying costs of taxes, interest expense and insurance. The location was so great that I knew it would work for some kind of business—but what kind?

As it happened, I had also bought a building nearby in Antigo, Wis., out of which I was planning to operate my restaurant offices, and it just happened to have a state-of-the-art automotive facility in the back. My plan had been to lease the service facility to a few mechanics and put a few cars out front for sale to generate some revenue. Since I was already considering getting my feet in the car business, I also contemplated putting a few cars up for sale at the Wausau location as a stopgap measure to cover the carrying costs of that property until I could develop a more suitable, best-use strategy.

As I contemplated implementing this temporary enterprise, I proceeded to research the auto industry through friends and others who had experience in it. I eventually became associated with a very successful retired general manager of a Ford dealership in the Green Bay area. He visited my Wausau location and communicated these magic words: "This is a phenomenal dealership location—and when I show you what you can do here selling used cars, you'll never build a restaurant here."

I bought into his enthusiasm, moved forward with all appropriate due diligence, and, in April 2008, opened Wausau Auto, a sales-only dealership, and, simultaneously, Antigo Auto, a sales *and* service location. I invested $1 million dollars in inventory, even though I had never sold a car in my life. People thought I was nuts!

The first six months went well, however, and were even slightly ahead of projections. But I couldn't have predicted how outside conditions were about to affect my new operation. It turned out that my timing couldn't have been worse, as gas prices went over $4 per gallon, Wall Street crashed, the recession hit and the worst time for the automotive industry ever in America suddenly arrived, all at once in October 2008.

Well, things got tough in a hurry, and financial risk is always a motivator of change. I set out to change the way I did business, as well as find ways to make my enterprises recession-proof.

THE U-TURN FROM DINERS TO DRIVERS

As you know, the title of this book is *U-Turn*, because it's meant to demonstrate how many car dealers were forced to rethink our business strategies after the recession hit. Well, I made a huge U-Turn when I decided to leave behind the old-school approaches to marketing and selling cars. Even with my limited experience, I knew that the industry norms of selling and advertising were not going to work moving forward. So, I went on a mission to find nonconventional methods that would differ from what other dealers used.

That mission began with me implementing the skill set I had honed in my successful restaurant business, a skill set that requires leadership, training, implementation, task orientation, customer focus and the ability to adapt and change quickly. I embraced the fact that I was an outsider who had just started in an industry that was suddenly struggling and decided I could use my lack of automotive experience as a way to avoid the "same is lame" dealership strategies I saw all around me. I wanted to operate my car business from a perspective that would *embrace* the current economic downturn, rather than try to fight it.

Well, my restaurant experience translated to the car business in ways I never expected. For example, the restaurant business is highly competitive, because there are many choices out there for customers who want to eat out. I learned a long time ago with my restaurant, Grazies, that you must differentiate yourself and provide compelling reasons for people to choose you over the competition. The reason I am in the restaurant business has to be the same reason that customers choose Grazies: to experience the fresh-from-scratch difference, celebrate life with family and friends, know that your money was well spent and be in the best hands in the business.

At the dealership, I needed to have compelling reasons for car buyers to come to my lot; I decided that those reasons should be because I believed everybody should be able to drive a nicer, newer car regardless of their past credit history and that no one should have to drive a car they hated.

In addition, the restaurant industry demands attention to detail, and the development of excellent people, process and systems. This skill set has served me well in the car business.

Other lessons I learned in my restaurant experience that have really served me well in the auto industry include the willingness to compete and be aggressively better in all areas than my competitors; understanding my niche—who I want to sell to; avoiding the temptation to be all things to all people; and striving to be the best in the area I've chosen in which to compete.

Surprisingly, many car dealers still do business the old—school way—advertising price and the car and then waiting for people to come on to their lot to buy.. They also rely on past loyalties, hoping that things will go back to the way they were before 2008. Well, I don't believe the economy will be changing for years to come, so I focus not on being a seller of cars, but rather a provider of solutions. I solve problems, for people in all walks of life, every day, and position my business to be recession-proof by giving people compelling reasons why to buy from me.

"WANTS" VERSUS "NEEDS"

People buy cars (or anything else for that matter) based on either their wants or their needs. Sometimes they just *want* to buy something (like a bigger TV or a nice piece of jewelry) and sometimes they *need* to buy something (like a new winter coat to replace a torn one or food to replace what's been eaten).

Since October 2008, "need" is the operative word. As I said, I believe everyone should be able to drive a nicer, newer car regardless of bad credit. Past credit issues are just one of the problems we overcome at my dealership every day, along with a lot of other potential problems, such as people owing more than their car is worth; being concerned about the value of their trade-in; having limited down-payment funds; needing a nicer, newer car because they commute and need better gas mileage; or needing a larger vehicle because their family has grown. Whatever the problem, we enjoy serving up the solution, just like at Grazies—and that's why we have hundreds of pictures of happy, satisfied customers accompanied by written testimonials raving about our staff. I'd like to share a few with you.

"I was very nervous before I came to Wausau Auto due to being ripped off by a previous dealer. I worried about finding a good vehicle that I'd like, and in great shape. Wausau Auto was great about everything. Very friendly, helpful & fair! Good prices! Nice rides! Awesome customer service! Thank you!"
— Candace Philipp, Schofield, Wis.

"I was stressed because of the economy the way it is, then I saw your cars and found I could afford a new used car. I'm not nervous anymore, I love my new car and can afford the payments. Antigo Auto took me through the process of buying the car and it was so easy. I would buy my next car here again."
— Shirley Slater, Bowler, Wis.

"Before coming to Wausau Auto I worried that I wouldn't find a good deal. But after finding my car I felt I had found one. Then, I was nervous about not getting approved for a loan. Wausau Auto did everything they could to get me a loan!"

"I was very happy with Antigo Auto, we had so much fun, and if there was anything that I thought was wrong with the car, they

fixed it. What I thought was really nice was they delivered the car for me at no cost, that was way too cool!"

— Geri Retzke, Manawa, Wis.

"I was worried and confused, my car had been totaled and I needed to find another at a time that I really didn't want to. I was worried about how I was going to purchase another vehicle before the insurance company came through with a payment. Wausau Auto allowed the time needed for payments to be received, even allowed me to use the car after the rental car time was up and until the reimbursement was received! I feel relieved and reassured I made a good choice."

— Janice Mayton, Wausau, Wis.

STEPS TO SUCCESS

In conclusion, I would like to encourage you to look at this short "U-Turn" chapter not just as a story about the car business, but also as a story of perseverance with valuable lessons that can help each and every one of you. Here are some "steps to success" I would like to share that may be helpful to you.

Be open to opportunities that are outside your comfort zone and rely on your current business acumen and skill set to translate into your new venture. You may be surprised at how well it does; mine surprised a lot of people.

Understand the economic conditions under which you operate and seek to recession-proof your business so that you'll still do well when times are tough and be prepared to maximize your opportunities when times are good.

Understand "the why": the reason you are in business must be the same reason that the customer wants to buy from you. Think it through and then provide compelling differentiation with clear reasons for why people should buy from you.

The journey from "basics to brilliance" is key: there is no substitute for excellent operations, people, process and systems. If you don't put the business basics in place and create a strong foundation, weaknesses will quickly make themselves apparent.

Compete and kick your competitors' butts! To do that, it's vital to understand the marketplace and your specific position in it. That means you need to know your customers, know your niche, avoid being all things to all people, and be the best in the area in which you choose to compete.

Always seek help; get training and education and surround yourself with others who are *smarter* than you, have a different perspective, and can help you think outside the box. That way, you avoid the "same is lame" syndrome and continue to grow and develop both yourself and your business. I have been fortunate through my own initiatives to be involved with the best group of people available to mentor me; they've enabled me to learn a lifetime about the car business in a few short years.

Never forget the importance of perseverance and implementation. You have to stay in the game to win it, and you must put winning strategies into action, not just hope for success to randomly come your way.

Understand what you are good at and what you're not so good at and learn to connect with your passion and what you want to do. Then, go out and hire experts to help you in the areas in which you are weak pay others to do the things that need doing but that you yourself are not interested in doing.

I wish every reader of this book the best of luck in all their professional endeavors.

About Scott

A true entrepreneur, Scott McCormick is a customer service and business systems development specialist who has honed those skills in the restaurant industry for more than 25 years.

Today he operates a successful restaurant concept called Grazies Italian Grill (graziesitaliangrill.com) where customers discover the "Fresh From Scratch Difference," and celebrate life with family and friends, knowing that it was money well spent. He also operates a real estate rental business, as well as two independent auto dealerships (199ride.com) where he is trying to change the stereotypical suspicion that exists in the car business and the bruised reputation of car salespeople. Scott believes everyone should be able to drive a nicer, newer car regardless of past credit history and no one should have to drive a car they hate.

Scott McCormick lives in DePere, Wis., with Kris, his wife of 25 years; and their three children, Max, Abby and Sam.

When Scott isn't working, he can be found in a hockey rink watching his kids compete or hunting somewhere in North America with archery equipment in hand.

CHAPTER 3

Customers Are Our Reason for Doing Business

By Joe Orff

I believe in order to explain Sport Chrysler Jeep Dodge's overall commitment to total customer satisfaction I need to start at the beginning and describe just how I became involved in the automotive business.

Many people who own automotive dealerships were more or less born into it. Their fathers or grandfathers owned a car dealership, so they grew up in the business and eventually took it over. My situation is light years from that scenario. Before I started working in a dealership, I had *visited* one maybe two or three times in my life, mainly when my father bought a new car once every five or 10 years.

So, how did I become the owner of a successful business, even though I started with little or no money and no prior experience in the business? It is an interesting story.

I was born in a small town named Pottsville in eastern Pennsylvania. After high school, I went to college at Duquesne University in Pittsburgh where I earned a degree in business administration with a concentration in accounting. After graduation I had basically no idea what I wanted to do with my life, so I answered some help-wanted ads in the *Philadelphia Inquirer*.

Because I wanted to live somewhere near Philadelphia, I looked for job interviews in that area and was hired by a large automobile dealer group as an internal auditor.

My job consisted of going to the dealerships and performing reviews of their accounting records. Until that point, I had never understood the complexity of a car dealership's operation or what a rewarding business it could be if it were run the proper way. After getting to know the people who were in charge of the dealerships and seeing both the good and bad ways their customers were treated, I began to believe I could run the business better than most of the people who were in charge and offer customers a much better car-buying experience.

I eventually became the controller of a large car dealership within a large dealer group. My goal was still to own a dealership, but I had no real money to buy one and not much actual experience running one. But I remained very interested in the actual aspect of the business in all departments, and in time was promoted to the general manager position. During this time I truly learned how to run a car dealership successfully, as well as how to treat customers well. While I was at this dealership, our customer-satisfaction scores soared from the bottom of the zone to a level that placed us as one of the top dealerships in the country in that category.

My success at that dealership led to an opportunity to become a partner in Sport Chrysler Jeep Dodge in Norristown, Pa. I started out as the operating manager and minority partner but within four years had purchased 100 percent of the store, becoming sole owner of the dealership. How did I do this? I focused on developing a total customer satisfaction process. When we sold a vehicle, we would take such good care of the buyer that the customer would find it nearly unthinkable to even look at a different dealership for any future automotive needs.

A CUSTOMER-FOCUSED PHILOSOPHY

Looking at customer satisfaction aspects of car buying and how I wanted to change those experiences was truly eye opening for me. In most dealerships, customers are not treated nearly as well as they should be. I set out to change that in my business. In my dealership, the customer is the only reason we are in business. Without our customers, there is no business. This philosophy applies to all the departments—be it sales, service, parts or administration.

We begin applying this philosophy in forming our hiring criteria. We attempt to hire people who are genuinely interested in satisfying the customer before, during and after the sale. To make sure we get the right people, we conduct an extensive interviewing process so that we can see if the potential employee has the ability to sell vehicles and the empathy to truly help people. This job should be about more than just a paycheck, although asking for and receiving a fair profit is tantamount to building trust with the customer and also vital to ensure the survival of the dealership. The bottom line is we want to have good quality employees who are knowledgeable about the product, knowledgeable about the credit required for the purchase and truly wants to help the customer make the best choice. We consider our people to be problem solvers, not product pushers.

Most people who come into our dealership are usually responding to some form of marketing like radio, TV, mail, or they have found us on the Internet. We have a business development center (BDC) that answers all inbound sales calls and tries to give as much quality information as possible to the caller and answer all questions regarding a purchase. The center also attempts to schedule a confirmed appointment time with the prospective customer to alleviate waiting time in the showroom. After confirming an appointment, the BDC passes on all information to a salesperson so that she or he is prepared for the appointment and has some appropriate vehicles ready to show the customer.

We understand that time is valuable, and we try to ensure that any time a customer spends at the dealership will be as worthwhile as possible. The BDC also attempts to answer all Internet inquiries within 30 minutes and provide as much information as possible to a prospective customer in a way that is as timely and professional as possible. Many times we have 15 to 20 emails between us and a customer as we answer all the questions that arise during the sales process. Any questions that we can answer before the customer actually arrives at the dealership are better for everyone because it can reduce the amount of time it takes to purchase a vehicle. This effort also helps eliminate any surprises that may come up as we get further into the sales process.

When a prospective customer comes into the dealership to purchase a vehicle, a salesperson will spend as much time as necessary interviewing all the people who will be using the vehicle to try to understand their wants and needs in the beginning. This process also helps to place customers in vehicles that are right for them. All customers have certain wants and needs based on how they will be using the vehicle, the budget they have for the purchase, and certain intrinsic needs and desires such as interior upholstery or exterior color. Buying a vehicle is something that the average customer does only every few years. We sell vehicles every day, and we spend the time to get to know every customer. We basically become a trusted adviser to the car buyer, not a salesperson.

After a customer decides what vehicle to purchase, we work exceptionally hard to find the best financing for the situation. In some cases, that means simply finding the lowest rate, but in many other cases, such as where credit is an issue, the process involves much more. We deal with more than 30 different lending institutions and can find a program for almost everyone. When the sale is complete, we introduce the customers to the service and parts department personnel, so when they come back for maintenance or warranty repairs they have a face to put with a name and feel comfortable bringing their car back to the dealership.

When we deliver a vehicle to a customer, we make sure the car is perfect both inside and out. We go over the entire vehicle to make sure the new owners understand all the features of their new vehicle and provide a full tank of gas as an added benefit. After the sale, we contact the customer every few days to make sure everything is working properly on the vehicle and learn if there are any additional questions or concerns. This procedure is done on every vehicle and ensures complete customer satisfaction. If any problems arise, we rectify them as soon as possible; this system also lets us know of any problems as soon as they occur.

In our service and parts department we operate the same way. When a customer contacts us about a service problem, we schedule an appointment that will be convenient for the customer and try to make that happen as soon as possible. When the vehicle is brought in for service, we diagnosis the problem and give a clear and concise appraisal of what is needed to repair the vehicle as well as the cost of this repair. We explain all necessary maintenance and attempt to perform this at the same time as any repairs, thereby minimizing down time on the vehicle.

The customer has three choices while their vehicle is in service. They can wait for the repairs to be completed in our waiting area which is equipped with Wi-Fi, television and reading material. We have rental cars available if the repair is going to take an extended amount of time. We also have a shuttle service that will drop off customers at their home or place of work. All of these options allow customers to minimize the amount of down time and inconvenience involved in having their vehicle serviced. In addition, we strive to repair the vehicles right the first time by employing properly trained technicians and doing whatever we can to have the right parts available.

TEN HINTS FOR A FANTASTIC
CAR-BUYING EXPERIENCE

Now that I have provided this background about my dealership and my philosophy about selling cars, I want to give you 10 helpful hints to improve your car-buying experience.

1. Do research on the Internet on the vehicle or vehicles you are interested in. The best websites for accurate and up-to-date information are the dealership websites.

2. After doing your Internet research, go to a dealership and drive the vehicle you may want to buy. Nothing can compare to the actual experience of driving and looking at the actual vehicle in the color combination you want.

3. Be honest with the folks at the dealership. If you have had credit problems, explain that up front. Every one will do better if they know all the specifics of the deal.

4. If you have a trade-in, bring in the vehicle and let a fair appraisal be done on it. If there are problems such as a reconstructed title or frame damage, it is better to be totally honest about it. In the end, the truth will come out. Honesty will go a long way toward getting a better value for your trade.

5. Find a salesperson that you like, who is knowledgeable about the product and who answers all your questions or finds the answers in a timely fashion.

6. Have a budget in mind for your purchase. Give yourself a range and see what type of vehicle you can get. But be realistic. A $30,000 vehicle with no money or trade down is never going to work out to $200 a month.

7. Loyalty means a lot to a dealership. If you previously had a good buying experience and that dealership has kept in contact with you, give it the opportunity to earn your business again. Many times you can receive more for your trade if your vehicle was bought and serviced at the same place.

8. Be flexible in your choice of vehicles, but always try to choose one that you like or love—not something you are just settling for. Most people spend a lot of time in their vehicles; they should be driving something they enjoy.

9. The lowest price is not always the best deal. Consider the total service you receive when you purchase the vehicle and whether or not the dealership will stand up to issues should they arise after the sale.

10. Shopping for and buying a vehicle should be a pleasurable experience, not painful like going to the dentist for a root canal. Enjoy yourself during the process and remember everyone in the dealership is there to help you. Make it as enjoyable as possible. Have fun.

About Joe

Joe Orff is a graduate of Duquesne University in Pittsburgh who has been working in the automotive industry his entire professional career. He is currently the owner and dealer principal of Sport Chrysler Jeep Dodge (http://www.sportchryslerjeepdodge.com) in Norristown, Pa., a suburb of Philadelphia. He is well-known in that area for his unique radio commercials, which highlight his belief that everyone deserves to drive a nicer, newer car and that he is a Dealer For The People.®

He currently resides in Phoenixville, Pa., with his wife, Linda, and their two children. He can be reached at jorff1@aol.com.

CHAPTER 4

How I Became "The Car Dealer Next Door"

By R.C. Hill, III

Growing up with a car dealer for a dad, I knew from an early age that a lot of car dealers—and even the industry as a whole—have a pretty poor reputation. So when it came time for me to start my own business selling cars, I knew exactly what I did *not* want to be. I purposed in my heart to be a different kind of car dealer ... to run my business in a different way than I had seen others run theirs. And that attitude has helped me survive some pretty hard times.

The idea of "The Car Dealer Next Door" actually came from my next-door neighbor. He's a really busy professional, and since he knew I sold cars, he came to me asking if I could help him with a problem. He wanted to get out of his commitment to his then-current car and buy a vehicle with more storage space and towing capacity. But since he owed more on his car that it was worth, nobody had been able to help him.

So I did the neighborly thing and told him I'd see what I could do. After listening to his needs, I got his car appraised, found a vehicle that met his needs, helped him find financing and had the car delivered to him. When it was all finished, he said, "Wow, I wish it was always this easy."

He has been a customer to this day.

That moment was kind of an epiphany for me—it was when I realized that people really want to deal with somebody they know, like and trust. And I wondered, why I can't I be that person who goes the extra mile for *everyone* who needs a car—not just my actual neighbor? Ever since then, I've tried to be "The Car Dealer Next Door" for every single customer who walks through my door, no matter where they come from. Just like with my neighbor, I see my job as helping each and every one of them get what they need.

LEARNING THE BUSINESS

My dad was in the franchise motorcycle and car business—so I basically grew up on a car lot. I got my first job at my dad's dealership when I was around 13 years old doing pretty much whatever the rest of the staff needed me to do. That meant sweeping floors, cleaning windows, helping out in the parts and service department—and picking up more cigarette butts than you can imagine. When I wasn't working, I still hung around the dealership, tinkering with my motorcycle and swapping stories with the service guys.

By the time I got to college, my plan was to try another line of work. I went to school in the Carolinas and studied business; my major was business administration, and I minored in both accounting and computer science. I assumed I would end up doing something in the computer field—it was the mid-80s, and the computer business was just starting to boom. But when I graduated, I didn't have a job lined up. My dad took my fiancee and me out to dinner, and I asked him if I could sell cars for him—just to make some money while I was looking for a "permanent" job. He was reluctant at first. I think he wanted me to try some other professions before settling down in the automotive field.

But after thinking about if for a couple of days, he said OK.

And the rest, as they say, is history.

I had never intended to go into the family business with my dad, but there I was. As it turned out, it was a good place to be because I really loved selling cars. So over the next few years, I set out to learn everything I could about the business.

I'll never forget the day, not long after I started out, when a customer complaint was making the rounds at the dealership. Actually, the complaining customer was making the rounds—he started in the sales department, then moved to the service department, and when he couldn't get anyone to listen to him, he demanded to see the owner.

I was in my dad's office when the customer showed up at the door, complaining about what was going on and that no one would listen to him. My dad invited him into his office, let him say his piece without interrupting him and then offered to go take a look at the car with the customer.

The customer had one of those big van conversions popular back in the '80s, with a cover for the spare tire on the back of the vehicle. He showed my dad that, under the cover, the spare tire was smaller than the tires on his car.

Now, that spare tire was perfectly legal and met all the basic regulations. But the customer wasn't happy with it.

So my Dad replaced the tire.

After the now-satisfied customer left with his new tire, my Dad explained why he did what he did. His advice was actually really simple: listen to your customers, let them say what they have to say, and once you have all of the information just do the right thing. That tire might have cost the dealership $70, but that customer would probably stick with our dealership for life.

And that lesson stuck with me for life.

ON MY OWN

I worked with my dad for the next 12 years, helping him build his franchises. Then I had an experience that probably isn't typical for most auto dealers' sons. My dad decided to retire, but instead of passing the business on to me, he liquidated his franchises. So I had to start over again, from scratch. I went to work for a public company for the next three years, until I found an opportunity to buy a Mitsubishi dealership in 2003. I'm proud to say I still run the same dealership today.

Getting started certainly wasn't easy. It was difficult for me to lose the momentum I had gained over 12 years at the same dealership. However, I did gain something priceless from my experiences there—I had already learned that my intention was to run a dealership based on serving my customers and meeting their needs. I knew my job was to listen to my customers and provide solutions for them. So I set out to run what I call a "customer-centric" dealership.

Of course, turning the dealership I had purchased into "my" dealership didn't happen overnight. When I first took over, I inherited a lot of the staff who had worked there under the previous owners. It's not that they were bad people—they weren't—but they didn't share the "customer-centric" philosophy that was so important to me. I didn't feel they were the right people for my dealership, but the next group I brought in didn't quite capture the spirit either. It ultimately ended up taking a couple of years of training my team members and promoting from within to put the right people in the right positions.

I got that all in place just in time for the economic downturn.

SURVIVING THE RECESSION

Here in Florida, the downturn started back in 2007—and as I write this, almost five years later, it's still lingering. What happened was unlike anything I'd seen before. It wasn't that people suddenly weren't interested in buying cars—traffic at the dealership dropped a little, but our reputation was solid enough to keep people coming in. The real problem was the people interested in cars weren't able to buy anything because the banks wouldn't lend them the money! Financial institutions got so picky with applications and demanding higher credit scores than ever before that it became incredibly difficult to get financing for almost anyone.

That's when I realized that if to survive we had to revamp the way we did business. But how?

I thought long and hard about our "customer-centric" philosophy, and what it meant to be focused on our customers' needs during this downturn. And I realized that, while we had always worked hard to provide great service when it came to selling and taking care of our cars, as far as financing went, we did what most car dealers do. We put the deal together, but once we sent it to the bank, our work was done—it was ultimately up to them.

Clearly, our customers needed something more. So we decided it was time to go the extra mile and actually get out there and help them find solutions to their financing problems.

We started sitting down with our customers and encouraging them to be brutally honest about their financial situations, taking that information into account when we put a deal together. Then, if the computer turned them down, we would call the bank personally and present the loan folks additional information to convince them to change their minds. This helped us get a lot more loans approved—and get cars for customers who otherwise would have been left behind.

MY FIVE PRINCIPLES OF SUCCESS

Today, my team and I still strive to consistently go the extra mile for our customers. I have a small dealership in a small town, and as "The Car Dealer Next Door," I have a responsibility to serve my neighbors. I want people to feel like they can come to me if they have a problem and I will help them solve it. So I have built my business on the following five basic principles.

Trust

If our customers are going to trust me like a neighbor, I need to trust that the staff I've hired to serve them will treat them right—after all, they're an extension of me. So I make sure to hire friendly people that will do business under our philosophy. They are all different people, but I trust that we're all on the same page—we all genuinely try to help our customers, and in order to really solve their problems, we listen more than we talk. It might sound strange, and definitely not like your image of a car salesman, but we actually sell more cars that way.

Honesty and Integrity

If I walk into the local grocery store wearing my shirt from the dealership, chances are someone's going to recognize me. When people hear my name, they might recognize it from my radio commercials or from my sign and associate it with my dealership. That's why I really believe what it says in Proverbs 22:1— that *"a good name is more desirable than great riches."* My name is on my dealership, which means that when all is said and done my name is on the line. So I make sure I don't do anything that will diminish that name or people's trust in me.

Do the Right Thing

You can look at 10 different things from 10 different angles, but most of the time, there's really only one question you need to ask: "What is the right thing to do here?" When you do the right thing, even if it's hard, things eventually turn out right. I've seen it happen time and time again.

There's a Solution for Every Customer

Every customer who comes to my dealership comes because they have some sort of problem—and it's my job to help them find a solution. So if they're looking for a specific type of vehicle, if they're having financing issues, even if the car they want to trade in is upside down, we believe every customer can have a newer nicer car and get great service. And we're dedicated to going the extra mile to make it happen.

Genuinely Try to Help People

It's amazing what you can accomplish when you put your mind to helping others. When you go the extra mile and dedicate yourself to finding solutions for people, they appreciate it and they remember you. To me, that's what it means to be "The Car Dealer Next Door." Just like the local doctor, I want to be the "go-to" guy that my neighbors can come to whenever they need help.

And word seems to be spreading. We have people coming from farther away—people who live 40 or 50 miles away drive have been driving all the way to our small dealership in our small town because they hear our ads. They come all this way just because they want to work with "The Car Dealer Next Door," but wherever they come from, I make sure my team and I treat them just like my next-door neighbor. We make sure we go the extra mile to find solutions that will put each and every customer in the newer, nicer car they deserve.

Today, our small-town dealership is the No. 5 Mitsubishi dealer in the country. Which makes me very proud of our "customer-centric" philosophy and grateful to my neighbors—even the ones who live 50 miles away—who have made me "The Car Dealer Next Door."

About R.C. Hill, III

R.C. Hill, III, is the owner of RC Hill Mitsubishi–DeLand. He has 20 years experience in the automobile industry, nine of which he has owned his Mitsubishi dealership. R.C. purchased the dealership because he has a passion for cars and had a desire to be a car dealer from a young age.

R.C. earned a business degree from High Point University in High Point, N. C. and is also a graduate of the NADA Dealer Academy. He lives in DeLand, Fla., with his wife, Mimi, and their four children. When he's not working, R.C. likes to fish, play golf and spend time with his family.

You can reach him at www.rchillmitsu.com.

CHAPTER 5

A Servant's Heart: Put Others First, and the Rest Will Follow

By Clayton Black

What does the idea of a servant's heart—which involves making a commitment to put other people's needs before your own— have to do with running an automobile dealership? It's certainly at odds with the image you typically see in movies of a car sales-man who will do anything and everything to get a customer to buy. Yet in my life and in my business, putting others first is precisely the attitude I strive to keep every day.

And I have to admit that serving others has served me—as well as my team and my customers—very well.

I learned the importance of service early in life. I came from a modest background—my father was the sole provider, and my mom stayed at home to raise my sister, my brother and me. When I was 15, I went to work for a well-known, local family restaurant, starting out as a dishwasher. I strove to do my job well; it may have been small, but it was still crucial to the overall success of the restaurant and the rest of the team.

Still, washing dishes is hard work—a lot harder than it sounds— and it didn't take long before I realized that I wanted to move up and out into what I call the "front of the restaurant." So I committed myself to working as hard as I could, doing my best to learn the tasks at hand, coming in early, staying late and doing whatever I was asked to do. And eventually it paid off—I was promoted to busboy.

This was much more fun than washing dishes—I was out where the action was and even got to interact with the customers occasionally. More importantly, my exposure to the customers I was serving helped me see how the work I did personally affected the customers and gave them a better experience.

This understanding only grew when I was promoted to waiter. Dealing with each customer face-to-face, I learned how vital each member of the team was to my overall success. If the dishes were dirty, if the food were cold, if the bathrooms were filthy, it would not matter how good a waiter I was. Without all members of the team doing their part, the customer was not going to have a great experience.

And since I approached my work with a servant's heart, I believed that providing a great experience for each and every customer was my job.

BEGINNING MY CAREER WITH CARS

When I was 19, I was hired as a sales consultant in the automobile business. It soon became clear to me that, just like in the restaurant business, I not only worked for my employer, I also worked for the customer. In fact, my real job was to serve each person who came to the dealership by helping them get the car they needed and wanted.

Because I had been raised to treat others the way I want to be treated, this customer-first attitude came easily to me. This is not to say I fully understood the concept—I sometimes forgot to approach each customer as a servant first and a salesperson second. However, over my seven years as a sales consultant, I still strove to abide by this philosophy, asking myself how I could best serve each customer—as opposed to asking myself how I could "sell them something."

Over time, I developed a large clientele and was helping more than 20 customers a month, which was pretty good in the car business. And then, after seven years, I was given a big opportunity: another dealership offered me a management opportunity with the potential for ownership. So I went to my boss and told him I was going to leave.

I explained the opportunity I had been offered and told him how my goal was to help other salespeople get to where I was and build a great team. Instead of letting me go, my boss asked if I would stay if he promoted me. I agreed, provided he would continue to allow me to advance beyond the initial promotion.

This was the beginning of one of the most important relationships in my life: my boss became my mentor. He took me under his wing and taught me accountability, responsibility, consistency, fairness, love and compassion for others; the list could go on and on. As with any boss/employee relationship, we had a few bumps in the road, but the love he always showed me made those bumps more tolerable.

I made it my mission to pass on what my boss taught me. As a sales manager, I tried to train my staff to put the needs of others first—that their job was about more than just selling a vehicle, it was about building a relationship with each customer. But, after about three years, when my boss promoted me to general sales manager, I let that philosophy slip just a little.

I got caught up in trying to grow our numbers to the next level. This was a good thing—our numbers did grow, and it's not like we were doing a bad job at customer service. However, the idea of serving the customer before all else was not always at the forefront of my mind. So how could I expect it to be at the forefront of my team's mind?

Eventually, I realized that I was not training my staff the same way I had when I was a sales manager. I needed to instill that concept of a servant's heart in my team of managers and let them pass that philosophy downward. So I reminded myself of my own servant's heart and continued on this path for eight years, until I was promoted again—this time to general manager.

FINDING MY WAY

Becoming general manager was a real turning point for me. Again, I started my new position focusing primarily on how we could sell and service more cars with the goal of making more money—instead of focusing on serving our customers. And it cost me. My first three years as general manager were a struggle. I pushed my employees hard, assuming they knew what I expected, customer service being the number-one factor, without actually teaching them to serve.

Then in 2006, we bought a new dealership—a store in a larger town only 12 miles away that had been our competition. This dealership had been struggling, with two different owners over just seven years and a less-than-perfect customer service record. I assumed that with our reputation for great service and our presence in the area, we should be able to turn this store around in no time.

I was sadly mistaken.

Running the new store wasn't easy. My plan was to work there every day while keeping control of the old store simply by checking in periodically. I was spread too thin, but this cloud did have a silver lining. In the attempt to turn our struggling new dealership around, I found my greatest opportunity yet to develop my servant's heart. Once again, I was out on the lot with the customers, dealing directly with the public instead of leaving those interactions to my staff.

And then, all of a sudden, a light bulb went on.

I realized that the way that I had built my business back when I was a sales consultant was the same way that I needed to build Keystone Ford. I needed to talk to my customers directly. I needed to make them feel important. I needed, above all, to dedicate myself to serving their needs.

After I came to this realization, things improved. Over the next two years, we slowly grew both operations by focusing on doing right by our customers—until the biggest economic crisis I can remember hit the country.

DEALING WITH RECESSION

Like everyone in the car business, 2008 was a tough year for us. We had no choice but to close down the old dealership, which meant letting go of a lot of good, tenured employees who didn't deserve being laid off. We relocated all of our remaining employees to our new location, which was a lot like putting a new blended family together.

That brought a whole new challenge—the struggle to get both "families" to work together as one. Again, I relied on my servant's heart to help me. I realized that whatever was going to happen needed to start with me, and that to bring everyone together, I needed to focus on serving each person who came into my life and my business—both my staff and my customers. If I was going to expect and preach this attitude, then I needed to live it and be the example of my own expectations.

I was able to pull my team together with one simple focus: just take care of the customers, always putting yourself in their shoes and asking, "What would I expect?" In my heart, I trusted that if we did this every single time, we would succeed at customer service.

I looked at it this way: with all the choices out there, why should a customer choose Keystone Ford? The answer was surely that we needed to be better than their other options. This isn't limited to car dealerships, by the way. When I think of both the good and the bad buying experiences I personally have had over the years, the difference always seemed to come down to the salesperson's *attitude*. When it was excellent, the service was excellent.

I began holding management meetings, talking a lot about attitude and the importance of giving unparalleled customer service. I stressed that every single customer signs our paycheck, reminding my team that, "If we want bigger paychecks, then we need to please more people." On my end, I knew that it wasn't just about treating our customers with respect, it was also about treating my staff with respect. With that in mind, I talked to my team and let each person know how important they were to the overall success of the team, regardless of what department they were in.

That focus on attitude in all areas worked, and I'm proud of what we've accomplished here at Keystone Ford.

CONTINUING TO SERVE OUR CUSTOMERS AND OUR COMMUNITY

One of my favorite questions for my sales staff is, "What is the number one thing a sales consultant should carry with them at all times?" I get all kinds of answers—everything from a pen to a business card and anything in between. But my answer is a little different. It's a pocket mirror.

If we had to look in that mirror before we answered every call, waited on every customer, or talked to every fellow employee, what would we see? Would we see a friendly, open face that the other person would feel comfortable doing business with? Or a face that is angry, disinterested or unhelpful? This principle doesn't just apply in business; it applies in life. Everyone is attracted to people who are positive.

I also feel that a big part of having a positive attitude and an important aspect of service is knowing and understanding our jobs. This might sound crazy, but I actually know of quite a few dealerships where the staff knows less about their jobs than their customers do! When we hire a new salesperson or service adviser, I make it a point, to ensure they are master-certified through Ford, even though Ford doesn't require it. I know it's important because if we are truly going to serve our customers at the highest level, we can never learn enough about what we do.

We also hired a trained staff of individuals in 2011 specifically to handle the technology end of our sales and service delivery. This was a major investment, but one I felt was necessary to serve our customers' needs. Technology has become a huge factor in automobiles today—the advances are amazing, but they can also be very confusing to most customers. I believe it's our responsibility to make technology easier; with a specialized technology team available at all times to help our customers with any issues they might have.

We even tell our customers that whenever they get a new mobile phone, all they need to do is bring it by and we will hook it up to the car—even if it's years after they bought their vehicle. As I see it, our job is to make sure all this new technology works for our customers—not to make them work to use it!

At Keystone Ford, service also means serving the larger community. I feel it's essential to give back to the people who helped you succeed, and we owe a lot to the surrounding community here. So we offer a free biometric DNA lifeprint every year, fingerprinting children so they could be identified easily if they go missing. We also conduct periodic seatbelt safety checks in partnership with the state police.

For several years, we have also conducted the Drive One 4UR School campaign, donating money to a local school in exchange for people taking test drives. We have also partnered with the local Marine Corps for their Toys for Tots campaign, donated to local food banks and given a two-year lease as a prize for a local teacher of the year. We consistently contribute to many other local fundraisers; and personally, my family recently helped another family that had children with health problems get through a difficult time.

Ultimately, I believe service is about making people happy. And that's one of the main things we try to focus on at the dealership—we want our people to be happy. If our employees feel loved, needed and appreciated, they do their jobs better, they serve our customers better, and we're able to serve the community better. We work hard to build a culture within our organization where we keep God first, family second and career third. It's not that we're here to preach to people, only to keep God at the center of all that we do. I truly feel that service is a cycle—the more we give, the more comes back around.

So what has our effort at providing the best service brought us? In 2010, for the first time in Keystone Ford's 29 years, we won Ford's prestigious President's Award. This award is not just about the number of vehicles we sold, but more importantly, the positive comments our customers have made about us.

I trust that this will be only the first of many of these awards, but that will happen only if we don't take our success for granted and remember to approach each day with a servant's heart.

About Clayton

Clayton Black is currently the general manager of Keystone Ford, located in Chambersburg, Pa., where he has worked for the past 23 years. He holds his customers in the highest regard and is dedicated to their satisfaction, committing himself to always approach them with what he calls a "servant's heart."

Clayton is also a 2006 graduate of the prestigious National Automobile Dealers Association (NADA) Dealer Academy and has been both chairperson and vice chairperson of the NADA 20 group. He also served on the board of directors for the Chambersburg Chamber of Commerce.

Clayton and his wife, Tamara, have four children: Brayden, Logan, Colton and Trevor. He enjoys spending time with his family as well as the occasional round of golf.

CHAPTER 6

Success Against the Odds: "Take Care of the People, and They'll Take Care of You"

By Lonnie Blackburn

Our customers work hard in their day-to-day lives. I know and understand that. I also know that the last thing they want to do is deal with a car dealer who makes empty promises and never addresses their real needs.

That's why we created Academy Cars—to be different, with different principles in place. When we started Academy Cars in 1981, my dad said something wonderfully profound that stays with me to this day: "Take care of the people, and the people will take care of you."

That quote has always guided our business philosophy. My wife, Joyce, and I recognize that we are nothing without our clientele. We understand that those who work hard deserve respect. We *are* a dealer "For The People®" because we *are* the *people*. In this chapter, I'd like to share how we battled against the odds to continued success and give you insight into just how—and why—we treat our customers with the highest level of respect.

HUMBLE BEGINNINGS

I learned to battle odds at an incredibly young age: zero. On November 6, 1950, I was diagnosed with "Blue Baby Syndrome," a serious condition meaning I most likely wouldn't be around long enough to walk or even talk. As a matter of fact, my parents were told I would only live for a matter of hours. That was 504,660 hours ago as I write this, and my 84-year-old mom is still counting the hours (and luckily, so am I).

Learning to work at an early age was helpful, and I wish more youngsters had that opportunity today. My first job started when I was eight years old. I worked for my dad, who owned a service station and tire center. I made 25 cents an hour working three afternoons a week and Saturday mornings, doing things like stocking oil shelves.

As an adult, my first full-time job paid a little more: $125 a week. Joyce and I had just gotten married, and our house payment was $125 a month! In 1973, I found my real calling at the local Chevrolet dealership. There, I discovered that I loved selling cars and building relationships with people.

I also learned how economic conditions outside of your control can really affect you. When the OPEC oil embargo hit, there were huge lines at gas stations and people were panicking. They were afraid gas prices would go over 50 cents a gallon! And here I was, working at a dealership stocked with all types of gas guzzlers: Chevy Impalas, Caprices, and pick-up trucks with big, fuel-burning engines. A new introduction, the Chevy Vega, became our best-seller! Imagine that!

A few years later, I teamed up with the person who was the perfect business partner for me, my wife. In October 1981, we opened Academy Cars, a small and simple car rental agency located in a strip mall in the back of Lawrence Auto Plaza. Armed with $1,400 cash, everything mortgaged to the hilt, and a $50,000 co-signed line of credit, we dived off the deep end. Yet again, the economy was not our ally. The country was in a recession, and the prime interest rate was 19 percent, if you can believe that. We were determined to make it, and with Joyce as my business partner, how could we fail?

To generate some initial cash flow, we advertised car rentals for $5.95 a day. We didn't rent to very many elite travelers. Instead, we rented to normal, everyday people like us. We even sold a few cars on the side to supplement the rental income each month.

That side business became highly important in 1995, when a national car rental enterprise opened a new branch in town. This competition put a huge dent in our rental business and presented another huge challenge to our survival. We had to step up our car sales dramatically. Sales quickly became our focus, and we managed to "keep on keepin' on." Like so many others, we have found our challenges have turned out to be our greatest blessings.

Now, Joyce never thought herself to be a "real" car salesperson, but while I was going to auctions and buying cars, she became just that. As a matter of fact, she was our top salesperson every month for four years in a row!

As we are all painfully aware, in June 2008 the United States suffered a meltdown of our financial markets and the Great Recession was in full swing. However, just as the Chinese word for "crisis" can also mean "opportunity," this time it proved to be true. We had an opportunity to acquire a former, and much larger, dealership out of foreclosure. Never being one to back down from a challenge, Joyce and I decided, after much consternation, to take the leap. We were selling around 26 cars a month in our smaller facility. Now, moving to a 14,000-square-foot building, the reality was setting in: continuing to sell only 26 cars a month would not be an option.

It was clear that our business model would have to change because we had to do things on a much larger scale. We had to learn how to serve our customers better and attract more of them.

That's when my dad's message really kicked in, "Take care of the people and they'll take care of you." I had to figure out how to make Academy Cars work as if it was on steroids!

CHANGING IT UP

Earl Nightingale, the late great motivational speaker and best-selling author, once said, "Look at what the majority of people are doing, and do the exact opposite, and you'll probably never go wrong for as long as you live."

We turned this sentiment into another great philosophy for us as we moved ahead with our major expansion. We didn't want to be like other car dealers. After all, I had started my career in new car stores, and I did not like the "game." We didn't want to traffic in all of the empty promises, which usually involve price, selection, value and service. Instead, we wanted to show how these promises could be kept.

Low price. This is a very prevalent empty promise. Dealers selling used vehicles buy them from the same places and pay about the same price for the same quality of vehicle. Finding a car way below the market value begs the question, "Why?" Instead of offering a poor-quality vehicle, we offer a higher-quality vehicle with our added value to back it up.

Selection. This can be another empty promise. Just because a dealer may have it on the lot does not make that car the best choice for you. However, Academy Cars has access to 20,000 different vehicles on any given day. If we are looking for a car that exists, at market value, we can deliver that car in a very short time span.

Value. Well, that carries many meanings to many different people. We feel it's an automatic component of what we do. The value at Academy Cars is "added" value to what you already deserve.

Service. Do you not have the right to expect good service? If it isn't delivered, it's a disappointment. Our service is clear from the time you walk in the door. Do not be surprised if three or four different people offer you drinks, popcorn, or even a warm chocolate chip cookie.

We have gone beyond the industry's typical games, slogans and marketing maneuvers in so that we can connect with people on a whole new and different level.

A DEALER FOR THE PEOPLE®

We wanted our customers' experiences to be fun, simple, quick and easy. We wanted to become a true dealer "For The People.®" For us, that means meeting people wherever their transportation needs are.

In the northeast Kansas market area that we serve, owning a car is critical to day-to-day activity. We put lots of miles on our cars. Without many public transportation options, a person needs a quality car to get around. Everywhere you want to go is a long way from anywhere you are.

The need for the right car is what drives customers to visit us. They have a transportation problem that needs to be solved in one manner or another. Though it's always technically true that the cheapest car to own is the one you already have, you can reach a time when maintenance exceeds interest cost, or a repair exceeds a car's value. Then, it's time for a nicer, newer car.

The new economy has caused all of us to re-evaluate our spending habits and hold on to cars longer. Because of this, new car sales had been slumping, and the salvage rate on cars was exceeding the build rate of new cars, by 3 million vehicles a year, obviously putting excess pressure on used car prices.

At the same time, many people have seen their credit scores hit hard. The average credit score has dropped more than 100 points in the past three years and more than 60 percent of us now have less than prime credit. At Academy Cars, we help folks repair their credit, finance their cars and drive a nicer, newer car at the same time. Life is a lot sweeter with good credit!

When someone comes in to see us at Academy Cars, we sit down with them and spend time talking to understand what kind of problem we're trying to solve.

- Is the Mustang going to accommodate the new member of the family in nine months?
- Is there a credit issue?
- Does an older car have to be replaced?
- Lack of down payment?
- Need a lower monthly payment?

Whatever the case, we desire to see each customer drive away in a nicer, newer car. More often than not, even if it does not seem possible, that is just what happens. As we always say, "Nobody should have to drive a car they hate."

THOSE WE'VE HELPED ALONG THE WAY

I believe that if you provide a solution to a problem rather than selling a car, you have a friend for life, not to mention a loyal customer.

This reminds me of many customers, including Derek and Lisa S., a couple from Ottawa, Kansas, who came to see us in 2006. When they were taking delivery of their 2001 Mercury Marquis, we advised Derek and Lisa how to restore their credit by making payments on the car in a timely manner. A year later, they brought their daughter in for a car and qualified to be her co-signer! They chose to make their lives better. Now, they can walk in and buy whatever vehicle they want—as evidenced by the much newer Dodge pickup Lisa just drove home this month!

Then there was a lovely couple, Chuck and Linda Y. They had been everywhere trying to get a car, any car. As they were getting the keys to their Buick LeSabre, we advised Chuck and

Linda—just as we had with Derek and Lisa—that the best way to rebuild their credit was to make timely payments on their loan. Three years later, when Chuck definitely needed a newer pickup, the couple had drastically improved their credit rating. They proceeded to tell *us* they would be diligent with their payments. Last year, when Linda's Buick needed to be upgraded, they came in with a great credit score, and she left happily with another vehicle and a credit union loan to boot.

Customer stories like these are why we love what we do at Academy Cars.

We have published our promise, purpose and mission statement, and car-buyer's bill-of-rights in print and on the websites, as well as displaying them in the showroom. The many, long-term, established relationships we have with our many lenders led to perfecting the "For The People®" credit approval process, securing approvals for more than 90 percent of our applicants.

As we have battled the odds over the years, we've been blessed to surround ourselves with great people. Without the best employees, you lack in all areas. When you are surrounded by people who share your values, ethics and moral standards, life is a real joy.

We view everything as a gift from God, and we want to share that gift with our employees and customers. I'm proud of what Academy Cars stands for and quite proud of all of our customers who have taken steps to improve their lives. And I can say that Joyce and I wouldn't trade a day of our lives for anyone else's.

About Lonnie

"Life is all about your priorities." And from a sermon heard at a Promise Keepers Conference in 1995: "God, Family, Career, and save something to keep yourself fresh! Keep these priorities intertwined as much as possible and most importantly in order of importance." This is probably the ONLY reason my best friend, business partner of 32 years, fishin' buddy, golfin' gal, Joyce, and I have remained married for 39 years!

To contact the Blackburns, you can email Lonnie@academycars.com or joyce@academycars.com.

Or call 785-841-0102 (work), or 785-691-8002 (cell).

To learn more about the business, visit www.LonnieForThePeople.com or www.academycars.com.

Visit Academy Cars at 1527 W 6th St, Lawrence, Kansas, 66044.

CHAPTER 7

Investing in People for Three Generations

By David Scism

People in Southeast Missouri have been buying their Ford cars and trucks from my family since before World War II. Founded by my grandfather Samuel Kent Scism in 1937, Sam Scism Motors (pronounced SIZZ-uhm) is one of the most recognized names in the local car dealership business. After 74 years and three generations in business, we still strive everyday to live up to our motto: "Our reputation is your guarantee."

In the early days of Sam Scism Motors, potential car-buyers could bring in just about anything for a down payment or trade— including horses, mules and cattle. My grandfather was eager to do business with the community and just wanted to make sure everyone who wanted a new car could get one—a belief my family still takes very seriously. However, sometimes in those days customers would also leave **with** farm animals instead— for a while Sam gave away a Shetland pony with each new car purchase! I am proud to say that even then he was employing innovative marketing techniques to put his business on the map.

Sam Scism was also unafraid to take a chance on people who might otherwise not be able to afford a newer car. Recently I met a woman, Gerri Pettus, who illustrated that point for me very vividly. She told me the story of her family's move to the area from Bloomsdale, Mo., in 1948. They had purchased the general store in Bonne Terre, Mo., and her father needed a new truck for the business. Because this man had been a Chevy owner his entire life, he contacted the local Chevy dealership but was met with disdain. They didn't know the new store owner so they didn't want to do business with him. Gerri's dad then called Sam, and my grandfather took him a Ford truck that very day. He was unable to pay for the truck at that moment since his money was still in the bank in Bloomsdale; Sam assured Mr. Pettus that his word was good enough and made the deal. Sure enough, Mr. Pettus paid my grandfather two days later and has been a faithful Ford and Sam Scism Motors customer since that first truck in 1948. Gerri told me that, at last count, her family had bought more than 20 vehicles from us. This is just one example of how my grandfather taught me that investing in **people** and treating them right will always pay great dividends.

A FAMILY AFFAIR

Although my grandfather died in 2010 at the age of 94, his influence is still felt by the second and third generations of the Scism family. My father, Charlie Scism, and my uncle, Kent Scism, are both key to the success of Sam Scism Motors. Each of us began working at "the shop" (as it's affectionately known in my family) from the time we were old enough to hold a hose and a shammy to wash the cars my grandfather sold. Some of my earliest, happiest memories are of playing in the cars on the showroom floor or hiding from my siblings in the boxes stacked high with car parts.

My father has run the service department for more than 40 years. We have thousands of loyal service customers because my father and the rest of his staff understand that people cannot function without their automobiles and are dedicated to getting them fixed them fast and right. My uncle Kent currently serves as president of our company and has been vital in implementing several successful public relations and marketing programs for the business, as well as helping people find the right car for themselves or their family.

We are also a very community-minded business. We believe in taking care of the people who take care of us. Not only do we donate "hole-in-one cars" to important organizations such as Kiwanis Club and Backstoppers (an organization that supports families of policeman and fireman killed in the line of duty), but we also provide a vehicle for our local food pantry to make deliveries to those in need. In addition, we loan the golf carts that our salespeople use to the local Relay for Life organization, which supports cancer research, and we also donate baskets to local organizations for various fundraising needs.

Most importantly, we are members of the local Chambers of Commerce in the communities we serve so that we continue to be cognizant of the needs of our area. These are just a few of the many charitable and community organizations we support. We are all life-long residents of this area, and our customers can rest assured that we are always looking for new ways to serve this community.

BLEAK DAYS

Although we are a successful family business that has stood the test of time, there was a period in 2008 when we thought we might have to close the doors for good. The economic downshift that was affecting everyone in our country hit us especially hard. People just weren't buying new cars—a new car was seen as a luxury by many, and the business suffered tremendously. In addition, we had just finished a $3 million renovation, and the money just wasn't coming in. The outlook for our business was very bleak.

But it was during that time that my family and I did a major re-evaluation of priorities and realized that we needed to be listening more closely to our customers. From that re-evaluation, we learned to not look at ourselves as car dealers who treat people right, but as businessmen who strive to make people's lives better. This was truly a pivotal period in our history.

This philosophy led me to create what has turned out to be a hugely popular local radio commercial, where I claim the title: "A Dealer For The People.®" The response has been overwhelming, and I believe that's exactly the kind of dealer I am. I'm a firm believer that if you treat customers with courtesy and educate them with the most complete information available, they'll be empowered, they'll be more informed, and they'll become your customers for life. I am also determined to put the fun back into buying a car and bring respect and responsibility BACK to the car business—a business that has garnered a reputation of being both scheming and underhanded. On the contrary, at Sam Scism Motors we are committed to giving our customers a positive buying experience that is rare in the automobile market.

USEFUL TIPS

Buying a car is a huge financial commitment; therefore, I want people to be armed with the most up-to-date and useful information when making that commitment. This is my best advice to those contemplating the purchase of a new car, truck or SUV.

Have Fun

When I sat down to outline these buying tips, I originally had "have fun" as my concluding tip; however, when I thought about it more I realized it should be my first tip. After all, who doesn't like to get new stuff? A vehicle purchase is probably the second biggest purchase we make in our lifetimes (after our homes) and let's face it—cars are cool. So when you go out shopping for new cars, have fun.

Often I see customers come in with a bad attitude about purchasing a new vehicle, and I attribute this to the historical negative stigma of our business. But if you choose the right dealership for you it should be an overall pleasant experience.

Ask Around
This seems to me like a no-brainer, but I often find folks neglect this step. Who better to tell you about their positive buying experiences than your friends, family, neighbors and coworkers? If someone you know, or better yet **several** people you know, had a positive buying experience at a particular place, chances are you will too. It shouldn't take much effort on your part to ask around or put a post on Facebook. I guarantee you will get several responses and people willing to share their stories with you.

Read Reviews
Get online and read reviews that others have to say about the business you are considering patronizing. If someone takes time out of their busy schedule to write a review, chances are that person is giving you good information.

Be Informed
Taking time to gather information ahead of time is a great idea. If you are buying new, be aware of factory incentives, pricing and any other information about the vehicles you are considering. Read online reviews of the model you are considering. See what owners have to say about their cars. Who better to tell you about a particular model than those who already own it?

Pay Attention to Facilities
You should be able to tell a lot about a dealership by its facilities. Now I don't mean you have to go the Taj Mahal of car dealerships to buy a vehicle. However, when you are at the dealership, look around. Are the showroom and service areas clean and tidy? Are the vehicles on the lot clean? What about staff appearance? Are they dressed neatly and professionally? You can tell a lot about a dealer by the way its facilities look. If they take pride in making the facility clean and pleasant, chances are they take the same care with customers.

Consider Dealer Longevity

This is a vital element of choosing the right dealer. If a dealer has been around for a long time that indicates they are taking care of their cars and, more importantly, taking care of their customers. You want to make sure they are going to be around to service your vehicles for years to come.

Learn about Services

What does the dealer offer outside the scope of just selling cars? Does this dealer also have a repair facility onsite or do they farm out their maintenance work? If you have to drop your car off for service, do they have a loaner car? If they don't have a loaner car service, do they have a shuttle van that can give you a ride or pick you up? Do they have a rental car services onsite or an established relationship with a rental car company in case you would have to leave you car for an extended time? Do they have a collision facility? In the unfortunate event you are involved in an accident, what better place to take care of the repairs than where you purchased your vehicle?

Expect Customer Service

This is one of the most important aspects of selecting a dealer. You should expect to be treated with courtesy and respect at all times. If you are not, this is a huge red flag that you are not in the right place for YOU. However, if you have heard good things about a dealership and you and the sale consultant aren't meshing, ask to speak with someone else or a manager. Sometimes personalities just don't mix. As a dealer, I would rather introduce you to another sales associate or my manager or assist you myself than have you leave with a bad impression.

Use the Internet as a Tool

This is a hot topic for me, and I could probably write a whole tip sheet for the Internet alone. Use the Internet not as a crutch in your buying process, but as a tool. Don't rely solely on the Internet to make your buying decision. The Internet is convenient because you can look at several cars in a short amount of time all right next to each other on your screen. My advice would be do some initial research on models and selection on the Internet, but go to the dealership where the car is located before you start negotiating on price alone—especially if you are looking at a preowned vehicle.

Every preowned vehicle has to stand on its own because no two are alike. Every preowned car has its own history, and quite frankly if I can SHARE that history with you, that car is worth much more than one I bought at the auction. Now, I don't want to scare people away from auction vehicles because we buy and sell them every day. However, that used car (whose owner I know and that was purchased and serviced in my dealership its whole life) is worth more than the one that simply came from the auction.

Buy Local
If at all possible, buy your vehicle from a local dealer. Not only will it be more convenient, but those are the ones who employ local people and put money back into your local community.

Locate Options
If the dealer you have chosen to do business with doesn't have exactly what you are looking for, ask him or her to find it for you. With today's technology the dealership can most likely find whatever you are looking for in just a day or two.

A RELATIONSHIP TO FOSTER

Remember, this is a relationship and a long-lasting one, so a dealer is extremely important. Also remember, the dealer deserves to make a profit and the lowest price isn't always the best deal. There are so many other factors (like the ones I've mentioned here) that must come into play while making the sizable financial commitment of purchasing a new car. If a customer makes a selection on a car based simply on the lowest price, what is that customer sacrificing to get that price?

Remember, buying a new car should be fun, not a chore to be dreaded. As long as the customer is armed with the most up-to-date information available and is selective when choosing a dealer that best meets his or her needs, the experience should be a pleasant and rewarding one for both the buyer and dealer. That's our goal at Sam Scism Motors, and it should be the goal for the dealer you chose!

About David

David Scism, better known in Southeast Missouri as "A Dealer For The People,®" is a third-generation automobile dealer from Farmington, Mo. His dealership, Sam Scism Ford Lincoln, is one of the oldest Ford dealers west of the Mississippi, having been in the Ford business for more than 74 years. David's goal has been to redefine the car buying process for his customers and to put the "fun" back into purchasing a new vehicle. To achieve this goal, David and his staff have embraced less-than-conventional selling techniques: the dealership boasts an arcade, a ping pong table, mini theater and even a gym.

To learn more about David Scism, and how you can receive free car buying tips, call Sam Scism Ford Lincoln toll free at 800-698-3177 or visit www.scismforthepeople.com.

CHAPTER 8

Why Choosing the Right Dealer Will Help You Drive a Better Car

By Tracy Myers

One of the most important decisions you must make when buying a car is choosing which dealer to buy from.

It may seem that all dealers are the same, but making the right choice up front can determine what car you drive and how much enjoyment it gives you in the years ahead.

Choosing the right dealer can mean you drive away in your dream car instead of settling for second best. The right dealer can make your life easier all the way through the process—from the initial financing to high-quality future service that gives you years of happy driving.

That's why one of my key priorities is making sure our customers have as many reasons as possible to choose Frank Myers Auto Maxx over any of our competitors.

I believe the best dealers go the extra mile to make it easy for their customers to decide to do business with them.

LESSONS FROM AN INTERVIEW

I was recently interviewed by best-selling author and legendary speaker Brian Tracy on his television show, and he asked me about some of the factors which make a car dealer special.

Following is an excerpt from that interview.

Brian Tracy: Welcome to the Brian Tracy Show and today we have a special guest ... Mr. Tracy Myers. He engages in something that you and I do all of our lives and he shows us how to do it better than we ever dreamed it was possible. So, welcome to the show Mr. Myers and tell me what exactly do you do?

Tracy Myers: Hey Brian, it's great to be here. I own a Used Car Dealership, Frank Myers Auto Maxx, in Winston-Salem, North Carolina. We specialize in helping people find, qualify for and own the vehicle of their dreams with little or no money down, even with less than perfect credit!

BT: Wow! So, if a person needs or wants a car, but they may have messed up on their credit in the past you can help them get the car anyway?

TM: Absolutely, we actually devised a special program that's unique to our store. It's called the "Everybody Rides" program. Our finance managers are called "credit miracle workers," and they work diligently every day to build relationships with banks and finance companies that no other dealership has. So, we are real proud of the foundation of our "Everybody Rides" program.

BT: So, a person walks in and they may have been turned down by someone else because their credit rating was not that great, what happens to them, what do you guys do?

TM: Well, what we actually do is try to secure the automobile loan first. Most dealerships try to show you a car, but you may or may not qualify for that car. Then they tell you that you can't have it, and you are really disappointed.

At our store, we do the interview process with our credit miracle workers and our non-commission sales professionals here at the store. It's a real easy process and, in 15 minutes or less, we can tell you—with an easy no-obligation preapproval process—exactly how much money you are approved for so that you can pick out a car.

BT: So it's a no-pressure selling process and close?

TM: Absolutely.

BT: You just work on making sure that you have the money, they can afford it, then they pick a car that fits into their budget.

TM: Right.

BT: Wow, that's tremendous, how did you get into this area?

TM: Well that's a unique story. My great-grandfather actually started the very first Frank Myers Store more than 82 years ago, so I felt like I had a lot to live up to. But, like a lot of family stores, I actually didn't want to get into the family business. I wanted to try something else.

Eventually, I came back around and came into the family business, and I bought the dealership from my father five years ago. And we were just recently named the number one small business in North Carolina—which we are real proud of.

BT: Wow, that's wonderful. Well, to be named number one small business you've got to have not only a thriving business, you have to have great customer experience, great people and a great reputation in the community; is that the case?

TM: Well, we like to think so. We have customers that have been coming back to us year after year for more years than I've been there.

BT: You know it's the most amazing thing but, in business, credibility is everything—and repeat business is the true measure of how well you are serving your customers. Isn't that true?

TM: Absolutely. And we try to provide a different experience and I think that we've succeeded with it. We like to make it a fun atmosphere, something that you don't see at a normal dealership.

We hear time and time again from the thousands of customers that we have helped. We ask them what they hate about the car-buying experience because most people say they hate it; it's just like going to the dentist. They say it's so miserable. So we try to make it fun.

BT: Well now, you have probably answered that, but what would you say was unique or different about your experience that makes it different from any other car dealership?

TM: Well, the thing in the car business—and it's really a dirty little secret—is that most dealers are trying to portray that we have special deals that we can get on cars. But that's not the case. Dealers buy their cars at the same place; we pay the same thing for them, and we have to ask what market value tells us we can ask for the cars.

It is all about the experience; it's all about the people. So, we have an arcade at our dealership—an "old school" arcade for the older kids—and we have an XBox for the younger kids.

We have a family movie night when we show movies on the flat-screen TV with popcorn. We have a free coffee bar and we have gourmet cookies. It's a different and unique experience. We like to think that it'd be a great place for someone to come and hang out even if you weren't shopping for a car.

BT: Oh, that's wonderful; it's almost like a Disneyland for buying a used car.

TM: Absolutely.

BT: That's great. And if you are a parent, and you have a choice of where you are going to go, you will go someplace where your kids are welcomed and well taken care of while you're shopping. That's a great idea.

So, here's a question, can you give me a story of someone who came to you, who had problems and challenges, and you were able to help them and they drove away with a car of their choice?

TM: Well, we can give you countless stories, but, here's a real short story. This was actually the first car that I sold, when I was selling cars at the store on a day-to-day basis.

A gentleman came in with his family and they felt down in the dumps. They'd been everywhere. Their only car had broken down. They couldn't get the kids to school, he couldn't get to work, the mom was staying with her mom and it was their last stop. We actually had them approved for a car and, in 20 minutes or less, they were driving away happy.

He just bought his 19th vehicle from us two weeks ago.

BT: Wow! That is great and I bet he has told all of his friends, and they told their friends, and they told their friends. That is the best business strategy I've ever heard. Make your customers so happy, they come back over and over again and bring their friends.

TM: Absolutely, and that's what we strive to do every single day.

BT: So, if a person was watching you and thinking they'll buy a new car in a situation where they can take maximum advantage of you, what advice would you give them?

TM: Well, I would tell them to shop around for a dealership which is reputable. It's all about finding the dealership, maybe not the one who has been around the longest—we've been around for a long time, but that's not the key.

Find the good guys in the car business—the ones that are wearing the white hats. They will be totally transparent and share all the information with you up front.

BT: That's great, we feel really comfortable with those people.

TM: Absolutely.

BT: What's the best way to find a reputable dealer?

TM: Well, the best way to find someone in the Internet age is just to look online or, of course, ask family and friends, because they're buying cars every day.

BT: Yeah, that's great. You know, they say that 85 percent of all marketing is word-of-mouth. People will go and check the Internet, but ultimately they listen to somebody they know and trust.

TM: Oh, absolutely, and we depend on that to keep our repeat business coming back to the store—perhaps it's for our noncommission sales professionals, and that is important to us.

We don't want our sales people to pressure our customers, so they are not paid the commission to our free lifetime engine warranty. The engine is covered for as long as the person owns the car.

BT: Wow! I have never even heard of that, that's phenomenal. So how do people get hold of you?

TM: Well, it's really easy. They can go to our website at www.frankmyersauto.com. There's a link there to get in touch directly with me. My direct phone number is on there, and there's a blog there that I write. So people can get in touch with me there.

Of course, if they're in the area, they can always stop by. I would love to show them around and introduce myself.

BT: Oh that's wonderful. Congratulations, Tracy.

TM: Thank you very much.

SEVEN TIPS FOR CHOOSING THE CAR DEALERSHIP THAT'S RIGHT FOR YOU

In that interview, I talked a lot about Frank Myers Auto and what I think makes us special.

But sometimes it takes a bit of time to get to know what a dealership is really like, and you don't have time to check out all of the dealers in your area when you are buying a new car. So I started to think about what someone should look for if they are making a decision about what dealer is right for them.

When you are making a choice, you need to find something that helps you make a decision quickly. Your first impressions will be important in giving you an idea about a dealership.

Although impressions can sometimes change over time, businesses that don't seek to make the right first impression are unlikely to try harder a few months or years down the line. So you can tell a lot from that initial contact.

Here are seven key factors you should look for to help you make the choice more easily.

1. Visit a Dealer's Website

These days the easiest way to check out a business is to visit their website. This can tell you a lot about the business and what it is like. That doesn't mean you should look for the flashiest website, but you learn a lot about a dealership from the information they provide.

If the website is not up to date or does not make it easy to contact a dealership directly, the organization probably won't be very easy to deal with. On the other hand, a website gets you off to a great start if it gives you the information you need, makes contact easy and appears professional.

2. Call a Dealer on the Telephone

The response you get to a telephone call gives a strong indication of what it's like being a customer of any business. Your calls should be answered quickly by someone who is friendly, upbeat and professional; he or she should be able to help you or pass you quickly to someone who can answer your questions.

Automated systems should be easy to navigate and let you speak to a live person when you want. If a dealership is not easy to deal with at the start, they are unlikely to be easy to deal with if you have a problem.

3. Visit a Dealer's Store

To really find out what a dealer is like, you should visit the store. You get a clearer picture when you see what kind of neighborhood the dealer is in and see what the building is like.

A good dealership should be clean, well-organized and easy to find your way around. When you arrive, you should either be greeted by someone right away or clear signs should show you where to go.

You are the customer so a dealership should make you feel welcome and comfortable quickly. Your visit should be a pleasant experience rather than a chore.

4. Ask How a Dealership Will Take Care of Servicing Your Car

Buying a car is an investment that becomes an important part of your life. You need to know your choice will give you pleasure and that you'll be able to rely on it. It's therefore important to know that the dealer will make it easy for you to get the best out of your car by providing convenient servicing and helping you quickly if anything should go wrong.

So find out about the quality of service a dealer provides—just asking the hours of the service department is a good start.

At one point, I realized that the operating hours of our service department were not ideal for many of our customers. While these hours were typical in my market—closed in evenings and on weekends—I was getting negative feedback about our accessibility, especially on Saturdays and Sundays.

So I began to keep the store open until 7 p.m. and opening it on weekends. Now that was not a popular move with my competitors. But the results were amazing!

Another issue I noticed was how inconvenient it was for my customers to get their cars serviced. They would have to drop off the car and then find a ride to get home or to work. So I realized that if we could help them out, it would be another problem solved.

I have learned that businesses which work hard at solving customers' problems are the best at building long-term relationships.

5. Ask What Guarantees and Warranties a Dealer Offers

Buying a new vehicle is an important decision, and you don't want to be stuck with one you don't like or that gives you unexpected problems. Something that seems like a good deal can quickly turn into a nightmare if things go wrong. You should make sure a dealership will stand behind its own product 100 percent.

So check that the dealer offers a money-back guarantee that allows you to put things right—even if you get home and find the car simply doesn't fit in your garage!

You should also expect a warranty that will protect you from major problems at no extra cost. We stand behind our certified vehicles by giving an exclusive LIFETIME engine warranty!

6. Ask How a Dealer's Sales Staff Are Paid

Even when a dealership offers a money-back guarantee, the last thing you want is to find yourself pushed into making a purchase you're not totally happy with. So make sure you find a dealership where the sales staff isn't too pushy.

The truth is many of salespeople are pushy because they work on commission. Our sales pros don't work on commission because we want them to be thinking of the best solution for customers—not about themselves.

7. Ask to Speak to a Dealership's Owner

A well-established dealership needs a well-trained and happy team to run successfully. So you can tell a lot about a dealership by the people who work in all the different areas—whether it's in reception, the sales area or the service department. In all parts of the business, you should find people who are friendly and helpful and can answer your questions.

But in any business you buy from, you'll always feel more comfortable if you can talk to the owner. You're not going to call them every time you have a question, but you want to know that they care about you and your needs.

While I could never run my dealership all on my own—and I depend totally on the great team I have around me—I want all my customers to realize that they can contact me freely whenever they like. Knowing the owner cares about your business can give you a great deal of confidence in the dealer.

These are just a few of the factors that can help you choose the right dealership when you are looking to buy a car. Finding the right dealership can determine which car you drive away in and will influence the pleasure and satisfaction your purchase gives you for many years to come.

About Tracy

Tracy Myers is commonly referred to as the "nation's premier automotive solutions provider." Best-selling author and legendary speaker Brian Tracy called him "a visionary to be compared to a Walt Disney for a new generation."

He is also a Certified Master Dealer and was the youngest ever recipient of the National Quality Dealer of the Year award by the NIADA, which is the highest honor in the used-car industry. His car dealership, Frank Myers Auto Maxx, was recently recognized as the number-one Small Business in North Carolina by *Business Leader Magazine*, one of the top three dealerships to work for in the country by *The Dealer Business Journal* and one of the Top 22 Independent Automotive Retailers in the United States by *Auto Dealer Monthly Magazine.*

Myers has been a guest business correspondent on FOX News, appeared on NBC, ABC and CBS affiliates across the country, been featured in *USA Today* and written for *Fast Company.* His inspirational stories and strategies for success are in demand across the country, which has given him the opportunity to share the stage with the likes of Zig Ziglar, James Malinchak, Brian Tracy, Mike Koenig, Bob Burg and Tom Hopkins ... just to name a few. His best-selling books help people become better consumers as well as inspire industry leaders to become "game changers." He was also featured in the five-time Telly Award-winning film "Car Men."

As the founder of his own marketing and branding academy, Tracy teaches ambitious business owners, professionals and entrepreneurs how to get noticed, gain instant credibility, make millions and dominate their competition.

For more information about Tracy Myers, please visit www.TracyMyers.com.

CHAPTER 9

Leaning on the Golden Rule

By Brandon Christensen

I grew up around the petroleum industry because my father worked for Mobil Oil Corporation when I was young. He also moonlighted in the car business. In the early 1970s, he applied for a dealer's license and began attending auctions so he could sell a few cars. He started out with cheaper cars and pickup trucks and gradually began buying more expensive ones.

It was fun to ride to school in a different cool car every week. It could be a Corvette one week, a Mercedes another week; I even remember a Rolls Royce he had for a bit. Of course, he always sold four-wheel drive trucks just in time for hunting season and the coming winter months in the Northwest.

The first few years of my life I lived in a suburb of Portland, Oregon. Nice neighborhood, and the economy in the late 1970s seemed to be going pretty well considering interest rates were rising and something called a gas crunch was going on. In the middle of all of this, dad was transferred to Los Angeles. He decided to try it for a few months, give it a chance. I remember going to visit him during spring break of 1980 so he and mom could look for a house and we could go to Disneyland. This was the time when the schools in L.A. were busing kids from the inner city to the suburbs and the kids from the suburbs to the inner city to attend school. My parents didn't like what they were seeing.

STRIKING OUT ON HIS OWN

Dad always had an entrepreneurial spirit about him, so in July of 1980, he resigned his position from Mobil Oil and sold everything he and Mom owned (except a 1964 Rambler American and a 1977 Buick Regal) to purchase a small petroleum distributorship in eastern Washington. This distributorship delivered fuels and lubricants to the citizens of the Yakima Valley.It was quite a culture shock for a third-grader to be uprooted from the beautiful green suburb of Portland and moved to the very dry 100-degree heat of the Yakima Valley. Luckily, the distributorship that Mom and Dad purchased owned a house adjacent to the warehouse. The house was a one-bedroom, one-bathroom, block house built in the early 1900s.

My dad always taught us about customer service. He said, "treat everyone they way you want to be treated." That is one of the basic philosophies that he had used to build his own business. It is one of the reasons his business has continued to grow since he and my mother bought it in 1980. Thinking back, I can remember many 100-degree, late summer evenings when my dad would grab our dog Silver, hop in his old 1970 Chevy truck (without air conditioning) and go check the fuel levels in the tanks of many of his farm customers. Certainly, checking these fuel tanks was a huge service to the local farmers during their busy harvest.

My dad spent every hour of the day making sure things were running smoothly. From checking the customer's fuel levels to driving the fuel truck in the evenings just to make sure there would be enough gasoline and diesel at the plant. Growing a small business in this valley was tough. He had to think outside the box constantly, just to keep growing.

LIVING THE GOLDEN RULE

What my father taught us about treating other people like we want to be treated has stuck with me throughout my life. Really, he was referring to the concept of the Golden Rule: "One should treat others as one would like others to treat oneself."

Most Americans think of the Golden Rule as something Christ taught in Matthew 7:12: "Therefore all things whatsoever ye would that men should do to you, do you even so to them." But this concept is older and more universal than a Christian doctrine. According to Wikipedia, the concept commonly called the Golden Rule describes a "reciprocal" or "two-way" relationship between one's self and others that involves both sides equally and in a mutual fashion. Its origins date back to the time of Buddha in the fifth century when he made it one of the cornerstones of his ethics and can be found in some form or another in many religions, philosophies and cultures.

My love of cars dates back to my early memories of my dad bringing another cool car from the Portland Auto Auction so he and mom could put it in the local newspaper to sell it. It was only natural for me to start going to the auto auction myself once I was old enough.

While in college, I attended the auto auction and started buying pickup trucks and SUVs. Using my dad's dealer license, I started selling a few cars via the local papers to supplement my income. It was also nice to upgrade my personal car from time to time. I remember starting out with a Chevrolet Cavalier Coupe and trading up to a Chevrolet Corsica. Eventually, I had a pretty nice Ford F150 that I had lifted with a fancy set of wheels and tires. Since I was using my own hard-earned money, I was limited to lower-budget vehicles. As I sold a vehicle, the amount brought in would be my budget for the next one and so on.

As I reflect on those early transactions with customers, I can remember many late nights and weekends answering phone calls and getting the vehicles cleaned up and ready for people to look at. Since I had virtually no overhead at that time, I kept my prices low. I didn't need to make a lot of money on each vehicle. My method always included telling my customer everything I knew about the vehicle—whether it was good or bad. Each transaction had to be a win-win or mutually beneficial transaction. This is the way I follow the Golden Rule.

GETTING IN THE GAME

My father became good friends with the local Dodge dealer. His name was Rick, and he had a very good reputation in the area. Rick had a partner who had helped Rick open the dealership but wasn't hands-on at this location. As the business became tougher, Rick and my dad discussed involving our family as a partner. Due to my dad's love for the car business and my knack for buying cars, boats and RVs, we decided that we would partner in the dealership and that I would be the used-car manager. This plan was extremely exciting for me because I would be doing what I loved doing, buying cars at the auction. My dad has such an entrepreneurial spirit about him that he was excited to see another venture take shape in the family business.

My responsibility started right away. I jumped in with both feet, buying cars I figured we would see a decent return on. Eventually, I could see that I had my hands full. It was easy for me to buy cars at below-market prices. The key was to also sell those cars within 60 days so we wouldn't lose money on them. It's all about turning your inventory. If a used car doesn't sell within a reasonable time, the wholesale value continues to drop. When the leftover cars drop in value, you take a serious risk of losing money on them. That money could be lost at the auction or by retailing them to a customer, but the bank will only loan against the car based on the book value (generally NADA or KBB wholesale values).

It only took me a few months to figure out that being the used-car manager held a huge responsibility. I would need to buy cars people would want in our geographical area. They had to be below book value, the right car, the right color, in great condition and something we could sell within 60 days. Believe me, that is a much tougher balancing act than it sounds.

Eventually, our partner Rick decided to go in a whole new direction in his life. This left me running the show. This was just in time to experience the financial meltdown, President Obama's election, the General Motors and Chrysler bailouts, and watch thousands of dealers in the country to lose their dealerships. Talk about stress. I learned a whole new level of stress. Oh, did I mention that my wife and I had a baby boy during all this?

Being responsible for running a Chrysler dealership in the midst of a failing economy, government bailouts and dealership shutdowns felt like I had been thrown to the wolves. I definitely was in a sink-or-swim scenario. Quickly, I figured out that having the right people in the right positions would make all of the difference. Unfortunately, finding the right people in a small town was difficult. Eventually, some key individuals were found for certain positions, and that made all of the difference. I found a sales manager who could hold his team accountable. He was able to grow his department in a profitable manner and continues to do so now. Service manager was another key position that I needed to fill, and eventually did. The service manager is key to holding the technicians accountable for the work they do on a daily basis. The technicians need not only to be accurate in diagnosing a vehicle's problem, but also to be efficient in fixing the problem. By making a few personnel changes and even downsizing a few jobs, we were able to maintain a sustainable amount of profitability to weather the storm. We continued to sell and service cars, trucks, SUVs, boats and RVs. We even added a couple of new boat lines such as Alumaweld, Sanger and Bentley Pontoons along the way in order to give us more of a presence in the boat market.

Trust and respect are a large part of this business. This trust and respect must be earned. Just because you open your doors and start a business doesn't mean the public will immediately trust your ability. Earning the public's trust and respect again moved back to the teachings of my father to treat other people the way I wanted to be treated. This basic principle has helped build literally thousands of trusting and respectful relationships in our region. As I reflect on the typical car salesman stereotype, I feel genuinely proud of how much we have been able to accomplish while fighting that stereotype.

Over the years, I have tried hard to teach my team how to be problem solvers instead of product pushers. Everyone out there has problems in their lives. If we can help them through some of those problems and make their lives better, it gives me hope that people will look at me and my dealership much differently than they see the typical dealership. My goal is to treat everyone the way I want to be treated and to solve whatever transportation problem my customers may be enduring.

Remember that each transaction must be mutually beneficial in order for the Golden Rule to be followed. Think about the many transactions we all go through during each week of our lives. Consider the trip to the local gas station where we fill up our tank. We pay for the fuel based on the posted price on the street which is normally not much different than the price at the competing station down the street. The station owner gets a fair price for the fuel, and we get our tank fueled up in exchange for our money. This happens every day at restaurants, convenience stores, grocery stores, auto parts stores, hardware stores, etc.

Think back to a time when you went to dinner with a friend and the waiter provided excellent service. The waiter probably kept the drinks flowing, made sure the order was delivered in a reasonable amount of time and also brought to you correctly. If you ordered your steak medium, the waiter made sure that your steak was pink in the middle instead of bright red or overcooked. That waiter who provided you with great service most likely was given a good tip for the service provided. Now, conversely, think about a waiter who did not provide you and your friend good service. Maybe you had to wait 20 minutes to place your order or your drink was empty most of the night—or worse—your order was brought out incorrectly and the waiter argued with you about it. Both instances have to do with customer service. One of these waiters treated you like he or she wanted to be treated. The other waiter either didn't care or was too busy to even realize the service provided was horrible. Obviously, the good waiter was following the Golden Rule.

As you can see, the Golden Rule can be applied in many situations. My father has instilled within his family and his employees that this is the best way to operate a successful business. I can assure you that this practice can help you in many areas of your life, including your relationship with your family, friends, coworkers as well as customers. I can attest to you that by following this simple philosophy your life will be much more rewarding and fulfilling.

About Brandon Christensen

Brandon Christensen was raised in rural eastern Washington. Christensen graduated from Brigham Young University with a bachelor's in business management from the Marriott School of Management. Later, he received his MBA from the University of Phoenix. Brandon has been an entrepreneur throughout his life. He has been involved in the convenience store and restaurant industries for many years. Currently, he operates a Chrysler Jeep Dodge Ram Dealership as well as a new and used marine dealership. Brandon has been a consumer advocate by providing transportation solutions to the citizens of eastern Washington. He has two children, Hunter and Kolby. He loves to hunt, fish snowmobile and go "Jeepin'" with his wife, Tammy.

To learn more about Brandon, visit his website, www.brandonforthepeople.com.

CHAPTER 10

Graduating to Good Credit: It All Starts with ABC

By Sam Snellenberger Jr.

It's always a source of pride to see someone graduate. You know in your heart they've reached a higher level and are now able to have a better life.

At ABC MotorCredit, we're very happy to have helped many people "graduate" to better credit. Having a higher credit score helps them obtain bank loans and better interest rates on other financing options.

You can see many of our graduates give their "commencement address" on our YouTube channel at www.youtube.com/abcmotorcredit. You'll also hear from a few of them throughout this chapter. Every one of these people needed a car for various reasons; some were in accidents that totaled their cars; others had finally gotten a job and were in desperate need of a car just to be able to get to work.

Whatever the reason, the bad economy delivered a double punch to these and many other folks in the past few years. Not only did the Wall Street meltdown cause the banks to freeze their lending practices, but many people lost their jobs and found their credit scores sinking as a result.

In most of America, people absolutely need to have a car. It's the only way to get around—whether it's to go to work, buy food or accomplish many other basic tasks. And we believe people ought to be able to get a vehicle.

That's the whole reason ABC MotorCredit exists.

"My credit was messed up so I went to ABC because no one else would sell me a car. I only had 300 bucks to put down and he sold me a Blazer. Everybody else wanted way more money than that. I got the car I wanted and a payment that will not break me. I also appreciate all my questions being answered without making me feel dumb. I just wanted to say thank you to ABC for keeping me on the road!"

—B. L., Canton, Ohio

"I bought my 1999 Buick LeSabre in September of 2009 from ABC and they were very helpful. Now with ABC helping me to rebuild my credit, I was able to buy a brand new 2011 Buick Lacrosse! Thanks for helping me get there!"

—T. K., Youngstown, Ohio

THE BEGINNING OF ABC

My father, Sam Snellenberger Sr., was the person who first recognized the problem of good people stuck with bad credit. More than 20 years ago, while he was working at a new car dealership in Cleveland, he grew tired of seeing customers being turned away day after day because they had low credit scores. He could see that they truly needed these cars and believed bad credit shouldn't be a life sentence of going without a vehicle. Instead, he believed there had to be a way to help these customers buy a car *and* repair their credit.

He reasoned that if he could provide these people with reliable used cars, they would be able to get where they needed to be and to get their lives on track. And, if he could provide the proper financing, they would be able to make the payments so they could not only keep those cars but also raise their credit scores and move forward in their lives.

Dad was from Akron, and he returned to his hometown in 1990 to make his dream a reality. ABC MotorCredit was born, and it soon began creating its first "graduates"—customers who bought a car, improved their credit and were soon eligible for the financing to buy new cars if they wanted. Happily, many of them kept coming back to ABC to continue to buy from us because of what we had helped them accomplish

ABC was so successful in Akron that we expanded; today we have four car lots employing 80 people (including myself and my three brothers) in Akron, Canton, Tallmadge and Youngstown, providing customers in northeast Ohio and western Pennsylvania with nicer, newer cars they can afford to drive.

Along the way, we've also built a reputation for treating our customers with respect and dignity and rewarding their unwavering commitment to success. Our programs have allowed our customers to be in control of their finances with specifically tailored plans they choose themselves, so they can finally see some light at the end of the tunnel.

And that's incredibly important after the difficult recession of the past few years. Today, more than ever, people simply need reliable transportation to get to and from work, to provide for their family, and to have some fun once in a while. That's a mission we continue to be excited about.

"The salesperson was awesome. Treated us with respect and was very personable. He explained everything to us and did not treat us like second-class citizens because of our past credit issues. We had car shopped a lot before coming here and ABC treated us better than anyone else! Great Service, Excellent Experience!!!"

—J. D., New Middletown, Ohio

"Like a lot of people these days I have found myself in credit trouble. I used to have little or no problem walking into any dealership and buying a car, not so much the case now. I saw this yellow sign on the side of the road and called ABC's number, half-thinking it was a scam. The following day I received a call from ABC MotorCredit and I filled out an application over the phone. Not only did they get me into a great car, they were also able to answer any questions I had. I plan on telling everyone about you guys!"

—S. B., Canton, Ohio

RISKS WORTH TAKING

By the way, when I say our customers don't have the best credit, I mean it. Our typical customer might have had multiple bankruptcies—or had two or three vehicles repossessed.

If the banks won't lend them money, you might ask, how come we will?

Well, the fact is a lot of quality people in America are in this predicament, especially since the downturn in the economy. More and more people ended up ruining their credit, and there have been a record number of bankruptcies and repossessions resulting from their hardships.

We faced our own hardship at ABC too because the banks that lend to us got very nervous after the economy crashed. It was harder for us to get access to the capital we needed to finance our customers' purchases. Luckily, our experienced management was able to put a pool of capital in place, so we could keep putting our customers behind the wheel of a nicer, newer car.

When a customer comes to us, we are never just about the sale but also focus on providing an opportunity for our customers to repair their credit. When they make payments regularly, we report those payments to the three major credit bureaus—even though this costs us money. Timely payments on a large purchase like an automobile are a great way to improve a credit score. That's an important component of the "school" they go through so they can become one of our graduates.

This process, of course, requires that we have good communication with our customers and look for creative ways to make it easy for them to buy a car. They have to be open-minded to what we propose, and we have to be flexible enough to make it work. All our staff members understand their roles as professionals, and we all work hard to solve problems for our customers.

This isn't to say a sale is automatically guaranteed to anyone who shows up at one of our ABC MotorCredit lots. We do have our own internal credit scoring process to make sure we don't assume too much risk. Otherwise, we would jeopardize our business and our ability to serve other deserving customers. But, after 21 years of operating our lots, we have a lot of experience in making the right decisions on who to trust.

"The experience was excellent. You guys were so great. I was walking and now I am driving!"

—*R. M., Doylestown, Ohio*

"ABC ensured I walked out with not only a vehicle, but one that fit my needs at a solid price. I figured I'd walk out with only one choice, that I 'settled' for something but I had a choice between TWO vehicles for my financing options. I never felt like I was being treated poorly, like I was second-class or 'getting the best I could for my situation' like I had elsewhere."
—P.G., Canton, Ohio

NOTES FROM OUR GRADUATING CLASS

We have helped thousands of people to graduate—and we're one of the few businesses who can say we're happy when we lose a customer, *as long as they are graduating*. It's not that we don't want to keep doing business with someone—but, when we can improve our customers' lives while helping them solve their transportation problems, we are happy to see them move forward.

Of course, everyone has a different level of graduation, depending on where their credit is when they start with us. It's also up to them to make the payments and build their scores back into the acceptable range in the eyes of other financial institutions. I can only say that we are there to encourage them every step of the way. We also make a point of celebrating their success, even though we may be losing them as a customer at that point. If you have improved your customer's life to the point where it makes such a big difference to his or her financial future, you know it's worth it.

Because we're a family-owned business and not some big national chain, we're able to take the time and effort to demonstrate our concern and do as much as we can for the people who patronize us. And I'm grateful they take the time to write us the many five-star online reviews that all four of our ABC Motor-Credit lots receive.

"I bought a car from ABC MotorCredit in Canton. My credit is bad and the salesperson listened to me and to what I had to say and helped me get the car I needed, after several other dealers told me no!! I didn't need lots of money down and he didn't ask for more than I told him I had and could afford. He worked really hard to get me approved before I even got to the car lot and made the selection process very easy for me, and got me a very nice car with a service contract. They will also report to the credit bureaus so that my credit will get better."

—A. M., Louisville, Ohio

"I was at my wits end!!! My brother-in-law gave me a clunker to get me to and from work, but it took its last breath on the side of I-77 during the last snow storm we had. I'm a single mom and have to get my kids around and get to work in something safe and reliable. On my ONLY day off for the week, I went to all of the car lots in the area and none of them would give me a chance. We drove by ABC motor credit at the end of the day and saw their sign for $99 down and thought we would see if we had any better luck. Even though I had bad credit, they didn't treat me like a lower person because of that—and they FINALLY got me into a car I could afford and that worked for me and my kids. I got a car a lot nicer than the one I had before and I am getting my credit built back up so I can do better for my kids someday. THANK YOU THANK YOU THANK YOU ABC—you have made a HUGE difference in my life!"

—B. G., Perry Heights, Ohio

These are the kinds of stories that make us proud of what we've built over the past two decades at the ABC MotorCredit company. These people were able to make the necessary "U-Turn" in their lives to get them back on track with a little help from us.

I'd like to offer final congratulations to everyone in our graduating class ... and we look forward to graduating a lot more worthy customers in the years to come!

About Sam

He didn't set out to be a used-car salesman.

Back in the day, Sam Snellenberger dreamed of being a skateboard star and set out to do just that. Directly after high school, he moved to California and devoted every waking moment to skating, even living in a school bus to save rent. It wasn't easy. It took a few years, but eventually skateboarding beat him down, and Sam put his tail between his legs, abandoned that dream and returned to Ohio to work in the family car business. But he brought home the most beautiful girl in the world.

The transition from skater–bum to corporate exec was difficult, and the girl soon left. This was when Sam realized he needed to commit, focus and follow through if he were to accomplish anything worthwhile. He did so, and it didn't take long for life to dramatically improve. He even won the girl back and married her. Skateboarding may not have worked out, but the hard knocks taught him the benefits of perseverance, creativity and fortitude.

Sam knew success would only come through knowledge, and so he dedicated himself to building relationships to develop a network of trusted mentors. Through this quest, he discovered an added bonus: business travel can be adventurous—satisfying his skateboard mentality. So he spent a lot of time traveling coast-to-coast and around the globe, learning from the best, visiting experts, sharing successes and failures—listening and learning.

He brought back what he learned to share with his family and grow a business success story. He is living his dream: he has the ability to feed his thirst for adventure, travel, and hasn't abandoned that skateboard dream, just amended it to include the successful chase of five AMA National Motorcycle Road Racing Championships.

Today, Sam finds himself a trusted mentor and spends more time giving to others. He has developed relationships with young businesspeople to advise, and he and his wife are two of the primary fundraisers for the Neonatal Intensive Care Unit at Akron Children's Hospital, committed to raising $1 million. Together they established the charity event called Walk for Babies, which has given more than $300,000 to the hospital so far.

Sam is most proud of the many lives he has touched and improved through his family business, ABC MotorCredit. What used to be considered a used-car dealership has become so much more in the lives of his community. Sam and his family business provide transportation solutions to people in tough financial places, while they improve their credit. And when many of these people successfully get their credit back on track, Sam is exceedingly proud of these graduates.

Sam continues to chase adventure, change lives back home in Ohio and give back to everyone he meets. He absolutely loves people who pay attention, remember their roots, are focused on family and learn from their experiences. Sam does not like lazy, incompetent people, or worse—those with such egos they are unable to learn from others. He also believes that Rollerblades should be wiped from the earth.

CHAPTER 11

How I Got Here (and What's In It For You!)

By Dane Gouge

If you would have told me back in 1983, when I graduated from Port Angeles High School in Washington, that about 30 years later I would own a successful automotive dealership, and be writing a chapter in a book about this business, I would have looked at you like a cow looking at a new gate.

It's not that I didn't have the ability or the drive, it's just that running a dealership wasn't anything that I had planned in my wildest dreams. But, as my story will demonstrate, life is full of surprises. For example, the summer after graduation, I suddenly found myself headed to college with an unexpected football scholarship.

I had spent that summer working full-time at my dad's tire shop. Now, this wasn't just your average ordinary tire shop that sold mostly to passenger cars. Nope. We catered mostly to log trucks and logging companies, so it was dangerous, hard and dirty work. Now with this college opportunity, I could go play some football and learn the ins and outs of running a business, which meant I could take over for my Pops when he was ready to retire. I was sure there was a lot of stuff he didn't know just because he never got to go to college. As a matter of fact, he didn't even fin-

111

ish high school, so higher learning would definitely be a plus. Of course, I needed a job to help pay the bills while I went to school so just take a guess where I landed? Yep, a tire shop in Boise, Idaho ... the more things change, the more they don't.

Well, I finished college, returned to Port Angeles and thought I'd make us a small fortune with all my newfound knowledge. I'd run our family tire business with a whole bunch of new ideas that would take us to a whole new level of success. But it didn't take me long to realize that college wasn't the key to making it with a local business and that there was a really simple reason my dad's business had survived when so many others failed, even when new competition was hounding us.

Are you ready for it?

That reason was customer loyalty. My dad went so much out of his way to help these small logging outfits that they stayed with him no matter what the prices were (not that my dad tried to gouge anybody). These rough-and-tough loggers would tell me, "We do business with your dad because he's always there for us. He lets us pay over time if we need to, he comes out and repairs our trucks in the middle of the night or whenever we might need him. He's there for us ... so we're there for him!"

And boy, they weren't kidding about that middle of the night stuff. I remember getting up at two in the morning to put a tire on a log loader or chains on police department cars because a sudden snow storm had come up. Whatever his customers needed, he was there to provide it (and sometimes I was too!).

SWITCHING GEARS

So how did I end up selling cars instead of tires?

Well, one of our accounts at the tire store was a local car dealership. They wanted to fix up some of their cars and trucks with custom wheels, tires and lift kits. While I was working with them on this project, I realized that the dealership did *everything* that had to do with cars and pick-up trucks. They sold them, serviced them, did body work and also customized them, like they were doing with the lifts, wheels and tires that we were supplying.

I was in awe, just thinking about all those new and used cars and trucks and everything that went along with them. You had so many more opportunities to make customers happy and grow your business that it felt like a whole new universe was opening up to me. I just loved it when customers came in to my dad's tire shop, threw us the keys and said, "Take care of it." They knew they didn't have to worry because their vehicle was in good hands. I couldn't wait to earn that kind of respect and trust from my new customers.

So, in the summer of 1994, I moved my family from Port Angeles to Centralia, Wash., where I started my new career as a car salesman. And once again, I was in for a surprise. On my very first day, the manager told me to go stand on the lot with the other 11 salesmen and wait for a customer and that if I did get a customer, I shouldn't let them leave until I got them to talk to him, or I could go ahead and leave *with* them.

That was different.

The only training I got was from what auto manufacturers called "source books." I was told to study them so I knew the product inside and out. As for any sales training, that just wasn't happening. All I knew were the sales techniques I learned from working at the tire shop which meant asking a customer, "Hi, what do you need?"

This wasn't the fun job I expected it to be. I felt way out of my element, and I was pretty sure the customers weren't all that comfortable with my inexperience either. It wasn't going well, and I needed to make some money at this for it to be a real career. So, instead of staring at the source books, I decided to instead study the most successful guys on the floor and see what they did to make car sales work for them.

That's when I relearned the secret I already knew! It was all about *customer loyalty*. The best salespeople had a genuine interest in their customers and their needs and continued to follow up with them after they sold them a car. They actually became friends with them! And that was just how I remembered it happening at the tire shop.

As a matter of fact, that had been the best part of working there to me.

That's when I knew my new career would be a slam dunk.

A couple of years later, in 1996, one of the store's sales manager quit. Well, I went to the boss and asked for that job. Another surprise—I got it! I was able to train my own set of salespeople and make the process work the way I wanted it to work. This sweet deal, however, just led into another surprise that was more of the sour kind—the owners sold the dealership the following year!

So we moved again, this time to Oregon, where I got a new job at a new place. Things again went well. I became general sales manager, overseeing the entire sales staff this time. But, once again, a big surprise hit. This dealership was sold too! The good news was that I was kept on and the even better news was that the new owner took me aside and told me, "If you keep on doing good here, I'll help you get your own store." Well, I kept my end of that bargain, and in 2003, after a few years of hard work, I was given the chance to buy the dealership. And that's how I came to run Astoria Ford here in Astoria, Oregon.

Now that you know how I got here ... let me tell you what's in it for you!

PUTTING THE SECRET INTO ACTION

The largest purchase made by Americans, other than a home, is a motor vehicle. It might be a sports car, a pickup truck, a minivan, or just an everyday, ordinary car. Once they decide what category of vehicle they want, customers have an endless selection of manufacturers, models and trim levels to pick from. The point is that customers are offered an incredible number of selections when they are car shopping.

One big thing I've noticed in all my years in the automotive business is that 98 percent of people buying a certain vehicle don't actually *need* it. They *want* it. They are really looking for a nicer, newer vehicle that represents who they are or want to be to the outside world. For example, someone who loves the outdoors and enjoys such activities as biking, fishing and hunting is usually after a four-wheel drive truck. A real estate agent, on the other hand, wants to be perceived as a successful business person. He or she might choose a nice, comfortable, highline sedan that has room for clients to ride along to look at homes.

Whatever they're looking for, after a customer narrows down their ideas to the type of vehicle they want, they face one more big decision—where to buy that vehicle!

The three biggest factors that go into a customer's decision on where to buy are location, brand and price. Car dealers advertise those factors heavily—so much that it almost becomes an even playing field. So the question for me becomes, how do we make Astoria Ford stand out? How can we be different in a way that really matters to customers and makes us their top choice?

Well, the secret that I learned at Dad's tire store hasn't really changed: *customer loyalty.* You just have to be good to your customers, and they'll return the favor by continuing to do business with you.

So how do you put that big secret into action? Here are a few of the guiding principles we have in place at Astoria Ford to make sure our customers know they're our first priority in everything we do.

TRANSPARENT SALES PROCESS = TRUST

This may be a surprise to you, but the biggest fear most people have when buying a vehicle is not price, but a fear of the unknown. Mostly finding out they got stuck with a lemon and having everyone tell them that they got ripped off by a "used car salesman." We want to make sure to put our customers at ease so they know that won't happen at Astoria Ford. So we have in place a transparent sales process.

What is a transparent sales process? It means we give all our customers all the information we can gather on the vehicle they're interested in buying—including the book value, the vehicle history report and any incentives that might be available, such as a lower interest rate on financing or a cash rebate. Once they have all those facts—as well as see the strong warranty we offer on our vehicles—trust is established, and their fears vanish.

GO BEYOND PRICE

It's natural and normal that a customer wants to pay a fair price for any product. However, people will always pay more for something when it includes an element of extra service that adds more value to the transaction.

The bargain department store might have the same clothing lines as a regular store, but you have to hunt for the right size yourself and hope it fits once you find it. At the regular store, however, a salesperson is there to help you. They'll bring the right size to your changing room and also give you experienced advice on what looks good on you and what other items might go with it to create an entire outfit. That kind of service is worth it!

The car business is no different. We make sure to offer extra valuable services to our customers, so they feel taken care of. Those services include free car washes, a powertrain warranty and other benefits that go above and beyond the price of the actual vehicle transaction.

EVERY SALE IS UNIQUE

When I buy a loaf of bread at the grocery store, it's pretty much the same as when anyone else buys a loaf of bread. Maybe one of us uses cash, and the other uses their debit card. One vehicle purchase, however, is always different from another.

For example, maybe Mr. Jones is buying a new Ford Taurus to use as the family car. Meanwhile, Mr. Smith is buying the same model strictly for business. Both the vehicles are identical, only Mr. Jones wants to trade in a minivan with 147,000 miles on it and he still owes $4,500 on the car loan, plus he has some credit issues. Meanwhile, Mr. Smith is simply paying cash. One transaction is very simple; the other requires some special handling.

That's why I make sure that our sales staff understands that every customer situation is different and needs to be treated accordingly. When there might be a problem with a sale, we work hard to find a solution. Every customer receives our full attention and effort in delivering what they want as far as it's possible for us to do so. Buying a vehicle is an important process to people, and we can't let them down on our end just because there might be a few complications to it.

CAR BUYING SHOULD BE FUN

When people go to the dentist, they expect a little discomfort. But when people come to buy a car, it should be a pleasurable thing, not an ordeal. That's why we make sure our showroom is fun!!!! We have a popcorn machine, as well as coffee, tea, soda, and candy available. We play music, and we make sure everyone has a lot of good energy to share with our customers. We want you to feel good when you come here—and we go the extra mile to make sure you do!

As I've mentioned, my life has been full of surprises. I suspect that is true for a lot of people. Even the bad surprises in my life have led to good ones, fortunately enough, with the best surprise being that I get to run a good, honest dealership with lots of satisfied customers. I hope you come in to visit and see the great store we've built up here.

And when you do, remember—the popcorn's on the house!

About Dane Gouge

Dane Gouge, otherwise known as "Captain Jeepers or Great Dane" from his fun and entertaining commercials, is the president of the Blue Oval Certified dealership, Dane Gouge's Astoria Ford. Dane graduated from Port Angeles High School and studied at Linfield College, Peninsula College and Boise State University.

He has been in the automotive industry for more than twenty years and emphasizes fun in his dealership.

Dane and his wife, Amy, have a mixed family of four kids and enjoy outdoor activities.

Dane is president of Astoria Youth Football and an assistant football coach at Astoria High School who also does the color commentary on the radio for the football team.

If you would like more information about Dane or Dane Gouge's Astoria Ford go to www.daneforthepeople.com or call 888-760-9303.

CHAPTER 12

Serving East Texas and Serving America: The Family Business Goes Global

By Kent Abernathy

In a nutshell, business is about relationships. Whether you're involved in Little League, a church, or a school board, you're not just helping your community—you're also building relationships in your community. So when people think about what you do and need someone to help them in that area, it's your name that will automatically pop into their minds.

Here in East Texas, I try to be that guy. At least as far as vehicles, service, tires and pretty much all things automotive are concerned. And of course, I enjoy serving my community as much as possible.

We moved to Gladewater when I was six months old. It's a small town with just about 6,000 people—the kind of town where everybody knows everybody. And the people here have had plenty of opportunities to get to know me. We're members of the First Baptist Church in Gladewater; I've been on the school board for seven years; and I was very active in the Little League Baseball

Association for 10 years, including serving three years as president. As far as the business end goes, I'm on the board for the Better Business Association in Tyler, Texas, and I'm also a member of several Chambers of Commerce in several East Texas towns, including Gladewater, Longview, Kilgore, Gilmer and Tyler.

So it's natural that, when people in and around East Texas are looking for a vehicle, or any sort of help with whatever vehicle they do have, a lot of them will think of me. This is my hometown, and I've built a lot of relationships here. However, the fact that I'm committed to East Texas doesn't mean my business is limited to East Texas. In fact, we've sold vehicles in Ohio, California, Florida, Louisiana, Illinois and more.

But we'll get to that a little later.

THE EARLY YEARS

I've been hanging around the auto business since I was a kid—it always intrigued me. I loved looking at the different car models and seeing how they changed year to year. And when I hung out at the auto dealership, I was hanging out with my father-in-law who worked there—before he became my father-in-law. I was close to his family long before I married his daughter. He and I played softball together and went to church together.

In addition to being interested in cars, I've always had sales in my blood. I truly believe you "don't ever meet a stranger." I like that interaction with people, the mingling and talking and trying to help people solve problems

Still, even though I loved everything about it, I didn't start out in the auto business. I earned a bachelor of science degree in technology from the University of Texas at Tyler, and I worked at what used to be known as Eastman Chemical in Longview, Texas, for 10 years. I also worked for my dad, and did some real estate stuff and some work in the specialty advertising business.

Until 1995.

That's when my father-in-law, my brother Mark, and I had the opportunity to buy the auto dealership where my father-in-law had been working for almost 30 years. He was the dealer-operator of the store, and working between my oldest brother and my father-in-law did have its challenges for me. There were different opinions and different ideas, but it also gave me an opportunity to finally work in and learn the business that I loved. Since then, I've done just about every job you can do at a dealership except for being a technician—only because I don't have the training for that!

Then in October 2008, in the middle of the economic downturn, my father-in-law decided he was ready to retire after 40 years in the business. My brother and I took over and decided it was time to put our own personal stamp on the family business.

TAKING OVER

The economy may have been down, but Mark and I decided we were going to grow. Of course, with six Chevrolet dealers within a 30-mile radius of our store, plus three or four GM dealers thrown in the mix, this was going to be a lot easier said than done. With 10 competitors selling the same cars, the market couldn't have been more competitive. Especially because we're in a town of 6,000 to 7000 people and so have to try to draw customers from other towns in the area.

But we took a leap of faith, right in the middle of the downturn; we added some employees and increased our inventory, even though just about everyone else was cutting theirs. We wanted to focus on customer service. Our dealership had consistently ranked near the top of the customer satisfaction scores for some 40 years, but we wanted to make it even better by making our dealership a more convenient place for the customer. So we changed our hours, staying open later and also opening up the service department on Saturdays and even on some holidays. We made the customer our Number 1 priority and aimed to give them complete satisfaction. That can be a challenge, but it's a challenge we're committed to meeting.

Sometimes, we take going the extra mile to the extreme. For example, I had a situation recently with a local family who I've known my whole life—my customer's dad was my mechanic when I was growing up. She was looking for a new Chevrolet Equinox at a time the model was in real low supply. In this small town, I didn't have the car she wanted, so she went to one of my competitors in Tyler to buy one. Did I like that? No. But she had to have the car right then, so I didn't have a choice.

Anyway, she recently was in Dallas, and something happened to the security system on the car, which died on her. She was with her son who was in Dallas to have surgery on his hand, so she was totally stressed out. She called several dealers in the area and was put on eternal hold—no one even answering the phone—when she realized she had my number. So she called my service manager; by this time she was completely (and justifiably) furious, saying she'd never buy another GM or another Chevrolet.

Now that's not what I want to hear. GM has a new focus now. The company is teaching us to do the basics brilliantly and exceed the customer's expectations. When this policy was put into place, my whole team sat down, and I explained that if someone comes to our dealership with issues—even though those issues may not be our fault—the minute someone trusts us with a problem it becomes our job to find a solution. So I knew I had to do whatever I could to solve this woman's problem.

I got the information from my service manager and called her myself. She was so upset with the way she'd been treated I could barely get a word in edgewise, until I finally said, "I want you to stop and listen to me. I'm going to help you, but you have to give me a chance." We sent her to an independent shop in the Dallas area and told her that, whatever the cost was, she should bring the bill back to us and we'd send it to GM so she wouldn't lose any money. Unfortunately, the shop that she went to couldn't help her—the problem had to be handled by a GM dealer. So

I called a GM dealer in Dallas who I had a relationship with and explained the problem; that dealership agreed to pick up my friend and help her in whatever way they could.

She called me two hours later and said she couldn't thank me enough. She told me the guys in Dallas were nice; they fixed her car and didn't charge her. That story demonstrates our philosophy—it may not have been our fault, but when she called and asked for our help, it was our problem. And we fixed it for her.

That philosophy, and that focus on customer service, seems to be working. We haven't had a down year in sales since before my brother and I took over in 2008; every year our numbers increase. There are 98 dealers, including ours, in the Dallas Fort-Worth Chevrolet zone, and there were fewer than five dealers who increased their sales from 2008 to 2009. We were one of them.

GOING GLOBAL

Another way we worked to improve our customer experience—and build our customer base—was by increasing our Internet presence. We were "on" the Internet when we took over from my father-in-law, but we weren't really doing much with it. We've since learned that 80 to 85 percent of people now do all of their car-buying research online. So we've worked to make that a little easier for our customers.

Today, we have a whole YouTube channel dedicated just to our dealership. We try to put three videos out a week on YouTube focusing on features of vehicles or specific models to provide additional information for our customers. We also got involved with dealer reviews, Google, etc. and developed a web presence in about every area you can think of.

And it's made a big difference—not just in East Texas, but all over America.

We've learned that when you get out on the web, you have a virtual showroom which is the same size as the showroom of your biggest competitor. That levels the playing field. Once that virtual showroom hits the Internet, provided you know your models and know how to properly showcase them, word gets out. And people come in—from some pretty surprising places.

For instance, we had a Volkswagen Golf that was a diesel with a manual shift. Almost as soon as we put the car on our website, we started getting calls from all over the country—it turned out this particular car was in real high demand. Within a day, we made an agreement with a buyer in Wisconsin, and he flew into Dallas to come check out the car. We sent a driver to the Dallas airport to bring him back, he bought the car and did the paperwork at our store and then drove it back to wherever he was from.

This has actually happened two or three times. We're in a small town, and we have towns surrounding us with a much larger population, but we're selling to the entire country thanks to our online efforts. And we're communicating with the entire country, almost like they're right here in our neighborhood. Just this morning, I got a "thank you" from a gentleman in Arizona for one of our YouTube videos explaining how to connect a Bluetooth phone to the car.

We're really reaching people all over America, all through the Internet. We also have an arrangement with two nationally known celebrities, the Duck Commander and the Buck Commander, who give us a lot of exposure. They come to our events here in East Texas twice a year, and of course, they're featured on our website. Plus, they drive our trucks wherever they are, which gets our name out there in all kinds of places.

It's a far cry from the way this dealership operated when it opened back in 1931. Our dealership celebrated its 80th birthday in 2011, and we've been at the same location since 1968. I bet none of the old-timers ever imagined we'd be selling cars to people from Wisconsin and chatting about features with folks out in Arizona. At the same time, we continue to be very community-focused— the Duck Commander and the Buck Commander were both here at the fundraiser we held to commemorate our 80th birthday—but today, we're reaching the global community too.

And we're still a family business at heart. My brother is president of the company and is in charge of the Internet marketing. My wife, Laura, is the first person you see when you walk in (she's at the reception desk), and she's also the beautiful voice you hear when you call our dealership. She also does the tax and title work and a lot of accounting. Even my 21-year-old son is now a part of it. He's been working for me for about six months on the fixed-operations end. My 18-year-old daughter is in college now, but who knows where she'll end up?

As for me, I run the day-to-day operations, deal with GM and the reps, plus handle service writing, parts, new and used sales, accounting—you name it. I know the place inside and out, and I'm proud to be a part of it.

We have a tremendous reputation in East Texas for being a car dealer that does things right. And whether you come to us from down the street or across the country, that's the kind of service you're going to get.

About Kent

Kent Abernathy is the vice president/dealer/operator of McKaig Chevrolet Buick in Gladewater, Texas. Born and raised in beautiful East Texas, Kent moved to Gladewater when he was six months old and is still there after 53 years. He graduated from Gladewater High School, Kilgore Junior College, and the University of Texas-Tyler with a B.S. degree in technology. He currently serves on the Gladewater Independent School District school board, Christian hunter and anglers board, and the Better Business Bureau in Tyler, Texas.

He is married to the former Laura Aaron from Gladewater; Laura is active in the day-to-day duties of the dealership, where she performs several of the office duties. They have two children, Aaron, who is active in the daily fixed operations at McKaig, and Blair, a nursing student.

Kent's hobbies include hunting, fishing, outdoor sporting events, and—recently—RVing. Kent says, "I am always taking flack due to wherever we go—I always seem to run in to someone I know. They tell me I never meet a stranger, and I hope I never do."

"I love the car business because of all the relationships you build with your customers," Kent says. "The interaction with the wonderful people that grace our business day after day, year after year, makes it all worthwhile. After all, everyone can have the same products to sell, but it is the customer service and your employees that make the difference. I like to think of McKaig Chevrolet Buick as being in the customer satisfaction business, we just happen to sell and service vehicles too."

CHAPTER 13

Yellowstone Country Motors: "Montana's Best Kept Secret"

By Manny Goetz

CARPENTER TO CAR DEALER

It was January 1 of 1997, and I woke up and told myself it was time to do something different. I had been a carpenter, builder and land developer for 20 years, and I was looking for new challenges. One of the projects I had been involved in was the startup and development of several Saturn dealerships in Northern Virginia. I was really intrigued with the one-price selling process and customer service that Saturn had developed.

I always had dreamed of moving to Montana and living in a log cabin along the river; however I still needed to make a living. I had spoken to a friend, and he told me about a dealership that might be for sale in Montana. So I packed my bag and headed west.

I arrived in Livingston, a small town of 6,000 located near Yellowstone Park. The dealership was in an old building. I was looking for a place to raise a family where we could be a part of "small town America." Livingston had the Yellowstone River running through it and was surrounded by majestic mountains. The dealership owners agreed to let me work with them until I could decide if I wanted to buy the business.

WHY THE CAR BUSINESS?

While I was growing up, my family and friends had always asked me to help them to buy cars; I was never too shy to ask the tough questions. I always wondered why buying a car had to be so stressful on the average person. I knew there had to be a better way to buy a car, but what was it?

I spent months talking to customers about what they liked and disliked about dealers. It was during these conversations with customers that I could hear and see the distrust that they had towards auto dealers. Boy, did I get an ear full. With all this information, I felt if we listened to customers' needs and treated them with respect we could sell more cars. After all, the customer is the most important person in our business. I always tell our staff, "The customer is the real person who signs your paycheck."

I was invited to a fundraiser in a neighboring town. As I was making my rounds meeting people, I met a dealer whose family owned several dealerships. He asked me what I did and I told him I was looking at buying a dealership in Livingston. He told me that none of the dealers in Livingston were ever successful. I told him I thought we could improve the customer service and create a more affordable pricing structure. He was quick to tell me that it was not customer service that got people to buy but the hype about the sale. He said our plan would never work and that a good dealer had to know how to control the customer. In his parting shot, he said there was not a lot of money in Livingston but more money in his town so folks could afford to pay more.

As I headed home, I realized that we would be the underdog when it came to selling cars. However, I still felt that customers wanted to be treated with respect. Our goal now was to show we could compete with the bigger dealers both in price and unlimited customer service.

GETTING STARTED

We committed to buy the store and started the process to get approved. We priced our cars so we could make a fair profit without the customer having to haggle to get a good deal. We committed to treat everyone with respect regardless of their income or negotiating skills. We met with the Chrysler dealer placement manager, and I told him we were going to take the hassle out of buying a car and allow customers to have fun in the process. He told me it would be hard to get accepted into the approval process with no previous car-selling experience but said they did like our business plan and attitude.

THE POLITICS

Our first obstacle was the dealers around us who complained that we should not be approved because we had no prior car expertise. However, to our surprise they approved us and told us some new blood would be welcome to the industry. They liked our ideas; however, they warned us that the other nearby dealers were tough and that it would not be easy to compete with them.

We went to one of the local banks and discussed financing. The bankers told us that if the current owner, who also owned the largest dodge dealership in Montana, could not make the business (then called "Cranky Ranky") successful that there was no way we could. I told the bank about our plan to make the customer number one. He said they were still not interested. We went back to Chrysler and let them know what we were running into. Chrysler officials said they had told me that it would be tough. With nowhere else to go, I called a lender we had used back east. This lender knew our track record and our strong convictions about customer service and decided they would give us a shot. We settled the next week.

Our first step was changing the dealership name from Cranky Ranky to something new. We decided to get the community involved, so we had a contest with the all the schools to come up with a new name. We would donate money to both the school and student for a scholarship for the winning name. The contest was a blast and a success. We chose "Yellowstone Country Motors." More than 300 names were submitted. Some favorites were "Get err done Dodge" "Manny Goetz you the car you want" and "Bear it all Dodge." The students and parents really enjoyed helping us pick a name.

LISTENING TO THE CUSTOMER

We found that listening to the customer and acting on their suggestions helped us grow very rapidly.

The first thing we did was to relocate the customer lounge next to the service and snack area and install a window. This allowed customers to see the work the technicians were doing on their vehicle and discuss repair updates with their service adviser.

We then removed the big signs that said "No Customers Beyond This Point" in the service area. Our staff welcomed customers into the shop to see the progress of their car's repairs. We find if you tell a customer that they cannot do something or try to hide something, you put doubts into their minds. We want our customers to know and see everything.

We also made it a point not to try to sell customers something they do not want or need. We listen to our customers and try our best to find the perfect vehicle for them. If they are unhappy with the vehicle, they'll be unhappy with us. There are several ways to purchase a vehicle with many different finance and lease programs. We train our team to find the best program for each customer.

We do our best to be honest with the customer. We tell our customers we are not perfect and if we do something wrong, we apologize and fix it with no argument.

We designed a 230-point inspection system on all used cars. Customers buy with the confidence that they will have a very reliable car. With this process, customer complaints are near 0 percent.

The plan paid off. The first month our sales went up. Within one year, the store went from selling 20 vehicles a month to selling 70 vehicles a month. Customers tell us they love the no-pressure atmosphere and that it was fun to buy a car from us. Chrysler has awarded us awards for service, fixing it right the first time and sales over objective along with the five-star dealership awards. AAA has rated us as a top shop. Our sales are made up of 60 percent repeat customers, which is far above the industry average. All this could not be done without a great staff of employees who understand that a customer's happiness is the heartbeat of our company.

GOING THE EXTRA MILE

When a customer is stranded and there are no parts available in town to fix a car, we will take parts off another vehicle to get the customer fixed and back on the road.

No one prepares for their car to break down. To help the customer get through these unpleasant situations, we provide free loaner and rental cars. In bad weather, our service department will pick up customers who need help. Heck, I have seen the service guys shovel snow off the driveway and sidewalk to help customers get in and out of their homes.

Yellowstone National Park brings in a lot of tourists with broken-down cars and they have a desperate need to get back to their jobs by a certain date. Our service staff will work overtime and weekends to get these folks back on the road.

We do a lot to help our customers. I have personally towed customers in. Delivered food in snow storms. Helped spread ashes of loved ones. Delivered firewood in cold weather. Delivered fuel and gas to empty vehicles, helped change tires, jump-start cars and even taken customers out to the river so they can catch fish. (That one is actually fun.) All in the quest to show the customers we are there for them.

We have seen all these deeds rewarded with referrals, great thank-you letters and many vehicle purchases.

SECRETS FOR FINDING A DEALER
WHO CARES ABOUT YOU

Use Common Sense

The first thing we learn in school is you cannot add apples and oranges. The same thing applies when you are buying a new car. Make sure that if you are comparing prices between two vehicles at two different dealerships that you are using the apples-to-apples comparison.

Some salesman will describe the vehicle they are trying to sell you as if it has all extra benefits and features, when the features are actually standard.)

The best way to make a true comparison is to get a print-out of details about each vehicle, lay them next to each other and compare each line item to the next. If they are exactly the same, then you can make an educated decision. If they are different, you need to adjust the difference with prices and then make your decision.

Look at Location

Take a close look at where a dealership is located. If it is in a high-rent area and the dealer has a large new building, this usually means it has higher expenses.

Common sense says the dealership will have to charge more to pay for these costs. Some of these dealers might get you in the door with some gimmick, but that is when you have to watch for the hidden fees. Some dealers add additional products to your contract that you do not need or agree to buy. Sometimes they will try to charge you higher interest rates. They have to make more money somewhere to pay their higher expenses.

Working with a small dealer who has lower expenses

should save you money in the long run both on the sale and with future service work.

Individual Dealers vs. Dealer Groups

We have customers tell us that the big stores they go to do not treat them very well.

It is pretty normal in business that if the owner is not at the store that the customer will not get the same service as you would get from an owner who cares and who is watching over the daily activities. Larger dealers have to sell volume, and to do this, they have to get you in and out.

At smaller stores, the owner knows the dealership has to take care of you—otherwise you will not return. In most large dealerships, you become a number and not a real person.

The myth that large dealerships get volume discounts is not true. I have heard salesman and owners of large dealerships tell customers that because they are large, they get to buy in volume. That is not true. Federal regulations require the factory to sell all cars to every dealer at the same price. So if you hear this line from a salesman, you know it is not true.

$99 Over Invoice or Similar Sales Attractions

Challenge them! If they advertise invoice, ask to see it. If you think a dealership is making up the invoice have them notarize the invoice and check it out with a reputable dealer. We have seen dealers advertise this way only to have customers bring in their price, which is different than what the real invoice is.

Remember, dealers with high expenses have to make the money somewhere. Every dealer needs to make a profit, but they also need to be trustworthy.

When a dealer says nobody beats their deal, we say run! Common sense says if they beat every deal then they would be the only dealer left in town. If you look around, I am sure you see lots of other dealers in business.

Dealers have to be truthful in their advertising and not mislead customers with hype. If a dealer advertises a guarantee, ask for it in writing. If they do not have it in writing more than likely they are trying to hide something. Dealers need to be honest in their representations and back up what they say.

About Manny

Manny started his career in the construction business in Virginia. By age 21, he had already received a general contractor's license and was building homes and commercial projects. In the late 1980s he was asked to be on the Better Business Bureau's arbitration board, which led to a seat on the State Consumer Service board of arbitration. He was able to see firsthand the conflicts between contractors and homeowners. He was asked to be on the board of the National Remodeling Council. He became a consumer advocate helping resolve issues between contractors and homeowners and quickly saw that the number one complaint with the BBB was unethical contractors.

With this knowledge, he became one of the founders of "Qualified Contractors USA," a free consumer referral service that helped consumers find contractors who were licensed, bonded, insured and had no outstanding consumer complaints. As an advocate, he was written up in the *Washington Business Journal* and *Washington Post*. He was featured in several TV programs on how to find a qualified contractor. He was a publisher and editor of *Your HOME* magazine. He was also the executive associate for several wedding guides and publications.

He quickly realized that the auto industry had some of the same problems as the contracting industry had. They were ranked number four with the BBB on most complaints. After discussing consumer issues with dealers, he found that most were set on doing business the old way. The only way he was going to help change them was to walk in their shoes. Manny was sure there was a way to treat customers with respect and still make a profit and has spent the past 15 years operating and working in a dealership.

From that vantage point, he could study the processes that different dealers use on customers and how consumers react. By implementing good processes it only took 30 days to see increases in sales and customer attitudes in his dealership. With sales increasing, statistics showed 60 percent came from customer referrals. He had dealers and the factory calling him wanting to know what he was doing to increase sales. When the market had its big downturn in 2008, all the other dealerships in the community were closed.

Manny feels that his dealership's customer service, sales and strong ties to the community are what kept them from the same fate.

Today, Manny is very optimistic that the auto industry is changing. He has watched many dealers change from the old way to the new way of winning over customers. He attributes this to dealers waking up and seeing that they were losing sales and becoming more open-minded to consumer needs. There also has been a lot of factory pressure plus factory incentives for dealers to be more customer friendly. Yellowstone Country Motors has won many awards for outstanding customer service. They have been awarded Chrysler's Top Five Star award and AAA top shop award year after year. Manny contributes all his dealership's success to having a professional staff that understands that the customer is more important than the sale.

For more information, call 1-800-497-1001
or email customerservice@ ycminc.com.

CHAPTER 14

Here to Serve: Never Make a Customer Half-Happy!

By Scott Lehman

When you want to buy a car, you're really out to solve a problem. Your family might have grown, which means you need a larger vehicle. Your car could be too old and may be worth less than it would take to repair it. Your credit score may be low, but you still need to finance a car somehow. Or it could just be a simple matter of being tired of what you're driving and wanting something nicer and newer.

For whatever reason, when you begin your search for your next vehicle, choosing the right car dealer to do business with can be a challenge. Finding one that will treat you right and appreciate your business isn't always easy. After many years of selling cars, I've seen firsthand what people go through just to buy a car.

At my car business, Premier Auto Center, we strive to give our customers a different buying experience—one that's simple, respectful and free of any high pressure tactics. It's what every customer deserves—and in this chapter, I want to provide you with some information to help you identify other car dealers who will deal with you honestly and with a genuine concern for your needs.

I've been in sales my whole life. As a matter of fact, I've seen myself as a "solutions provider" since I was seven years old. When you grow up in Arizona, you get used to the occasional dust storm blowing through town. Well, when I was a kid, many of our older neighbors weren't in good enough physical shape to get out and sweep away the dirt those storms dumped on their carports, so I did it for them—and that's how I started making some ice cream money (ice cream is the key to surviving the Arizona heat, you know!).

As I got older, I made macramé plant hangers (all the rage in the '70s) and sold them door-to-door. A local crafts store eventually gave me space to sell them at their location—it became kind of my first "dealership." I had a store within a store. Keep that concept in mind as you read.

My string of minor sales successes finally hit its first big hurdle when I was in the Army. I tried selling life insurance door-to-door, but maybe I should have stuck to macramé, because I never sold one single policy. The only goal I really reached was someone finally agreeing to let me make a presentation. Other than that, the sound of slamming doors still rings in my ears to this day.

That's where I really learned that you shouldn't take rejection personally, that it's best to just move on to the next challenge. After I served my time in the military, I ended up back in my home town of Casa Grande, working in my father's appliance store, Lehman's Appliance. And that's where I learned my second big sales lesson, which was my father's mantra: "Never make a customer half-happy. It serves no purpose."

Every day when I come to work at my dealership, Premier Auto Center, I keep that thought front and center in everything I do. When my dad said it to me, it just made complete sense. What good are half-happy customers? You should either try to make them completely happy or not at all. Happy customers feel their needs were met, if not surpassed, and they feel motivated to return to buy again when necessary. Half-happy customers? Well, they think of you with a shrug. "Yeah ... that place is OK, I guess," is not the kind of ringing endorsement you build a business with.

FROM APPLIANCES TO CARS

I went from working for my father to working for myself. It was 1994; I was a stay-at-home dad, taking care of our twins, and selling software systems out of the house (not the most lucrative gig in the world), when an old friend recruited me into the car business. He told me I should really try it out, and it turned out he was very right, because I was immediately comfortable doing it. So comfortable that I actually ended up selling a couple of cars before I officially started at the dealership.

That's because I loved selling cars. It was a whole different feeling than selling appliances at my dad's store. People don't get that excited about buying a washing machine, to be honest. Cars are more of an emotional and, ideally, fun purchase. They make a difference in people's lives and I became hooked on making that difference as positive as possible.

That, in turn, meant I double downed on my determination to never make a customer half-happy. That meant I did things other car salesmen probably wouldn't even consider doing. For example, maybe a customer that I had sold a car to in the past would come see me again, and say this time, he wanted to buy a Nissan. Well, even if I didn't sell Nissans, I would go out and get that Nissan, bring it back to the lot where I worked and sell it to him. I would usually make zero on the deal, but I knew that person would come back to me the next time he needed a car (and, in the meantime, he wouldn't be meeting a Nissan car salesman that he might like better!). That kind of effort may sound crazy, but I do believe that's what made me successful at my job and how I created so much long-term customer loyalty.

I sold vehicles at a few different places during my first years as a car salesman and worked on building up my customer list.

Finally, I was asked by one dealership what I wanted to stay put. I thought about it and gave them my answer: "You give me a room, don't put a manager over my head and let me do my own deals. I don't need to talk to your customers; I'll be working with my own."

Well, they gave me that room and I operated as a dealership within a dealership (just like I did with my macramé plant hangers back when I was 13). I had my own little inventory of about 15 cars; I did my own advertising; I continued to grow my base of customers; and I got my feet wet running my own car business in the best possible (and most low-risk) way. It was great to sell cars the way I wanted to sell them, by putting the customer first, and it was awesome to see my success grow through this simple principle.

THE BIRTH (AND NEAR-DEATH) OF PREMIER AUTO CENTER

That's why, when I was given the opportunity to run my own dealership, Premier Auto Center, it seemed like the perfect time to make the leap to a larger operation. I knew if I could create the kind of culture and organization that reflected my customer-centric philosophy, then we could be successful at what we do. I reminded everyone on my new team to keep an eye on long-term success, not short-term gain. That, of course, meant no customer could be left half-happy!

It was late 2007 when we opened our doors, and the economy was going great. We started off strong, by selling a lot of cars, more than the nearby new-car stores. Still, something nagged at me, and for some reason, I felt as if I was walking towards a cliff in the fog. I knew that cliff was somewhere out there in front of me, but I didn't know where.

In October of 2008, I found that cliff—not that I wanted to—when the "Great Recession" kicked in and caused us to take a long, hard fall.

Luckily enough, prior to the downturn, we had done well enough and made enough customers happy to get us through the tough months ahead.

"HOW CAN I HELP?"

We all know that many businesses went under during the last several years, including more than a few car dealers. I believe a large reason that we rode out the storm is because we never forgot our role as a "solutions provider" and always maintained the philosophy of "start solving & stop selling." Now, many salespeople don't like this mindset. They don't like to think of themselves as serving the customer instead of selling the customer. But I really insist that we all look at customers differently at Premier, and thankfully, all my sales staff have gotten on board with this new way of thinking.

As I mentioned at the beginning of this chapter, when someone shows up at our store, they're coming with a transportation issue that needs to be addressed. The important thing is to talk with them—*really* talk with them—figure out what the problem is and present solutions. If you present enough solutions, you're going to be able to find their specific answer, even when their problem seems insolvable.

For example, the bad economy caused a lot of people who owned their cars to take out high-interest title loans. The actual loan total may not have been all that much, but because of the accumulating interest, the payments wound up being a lot. A woman who wanted to buy one of our cars was struggling with a payment of more than $700 a month on her current car and didn't know how to get out of it. Well, we helped her refinance the payment, cutting it down by more than $400 and helping her buy a nicer, newer car. Nobody else went to that trouble for her, but we wanted to make sure to find her the right solution to help her get what she wanted.

There was another young guy who had been dismissed by the other car dealers because of *his* problem, which was the older

Chevy Camaro that he owned and literally couldn't drive. It was incapable of passing an emissions test, and in Arizona, if your car doesn't pass the emissions test, you can't register it with the state. He was desperate to get rid of it and get into a car he *could* drive. Very understandable! No dealer, however, wanted to take the Camaro as a trade-in.

We did. We helped him buy a car that passed the emissions test and took his Camaro and resold it where emissions tests weren't required. He was incredibly grateful because nobody else had sat down with him to *find a solution.*

FINDING THE RIGHT DEALER

I saw a lot during my years working at established dealerships. A lot I didn't like. Hard-sell tactics that were more about dealer profits than customer needs didn't sit well with me. That's why I never committed fully to one store until I was sure I could act as independently as possible and why I currently run my own dealership in a completely different style.

Buying a car shouldn't be a tense negotiation where the customer is never sure what the truth is. The fact is that virtually everyone will buy a new or used car at some point in their life from a dealer. When they go through a brutal sales process, they're likely not to return to the same dealer. It's my dad's principle in action; the customer may go home half-happy, only because they got the car they wanted, but they're not going to be anxious to return to the place that didn't treat them with the respect they expect when they make a large purchase.

It doesn't really cost more to do business with a service attitude in place. It may take a little more effort and time, but that effort and time is consistently paid back in the form of return business. Being a solutions provider isn't a new concept but actually a lost art. Our parents and grandparents had this type of relationship with the local retailers and service companies of their time. They were more a part of the community and felt more of a responsibility to serve it well. It was good citizenship and good business. It's definitely more of a challenge to do that with a modern-day store because it's a little more difficult to find the right people who share this philosophy. But I was determined to do it.

I firmly believe that the customer's car-buying experience should be:

- Pleasant

- Simple and clear

- Free of manipulation and high-pressure tactics

- Respectful

- Memorable in a positive way.

That may seem like an impossible list to fulfill, but there are other dealers like myself who are anxious to deliver all those elements to the car-buying process. And when they are delivered, you'll find that you're able to make better, more reasoned decisions because you're less stressed.

How do you find a car dealer of this type? Well, when you visit a dealership, see which of the following things happen when salespeople approach you:

Do they ask you questions about what your actual needs are, instead of showing you cars immediately without much conversation? Are they willing to explore solutions when you have an unusual problem to overcome?

Do they allow you time to think things over without pushing you to decide too soon about a car that interests you? Are they clear about the cost of a car, instead of confusing you about how much you would actually pay for it? Are they showing you the type of car you want, instead of pushing you into a more expensive car or another one they're just trying to get rid of?

If you answered "yes" to the above questions, you're most likely in good hands.

I've come a long way from sweeping the dirt from my neighbors' carports, but I still care about doing the best possible job for my customers. Being a "solutions provider" instead of a salesman provides me with peace of mind because I know that I have dealt as fairly and ethically as possible with people who patronize my business. If you live in the area and haven't visited us at Premier Auto Center, I invite you to come on down and see for yourself how well you're treated.

I guarantee you won't leave half-happy.

About Scott

 Scott Lehman, the owner of Premier Auto Center in Casa Grande and Tucson, Arizona, is a successful car dealer as well as a best-selling author on the topic of changing the customer experience of car buying. Growing up in a small community and working in the family business with a dad who knew the value of a customer, Scott learned first-hand what it takes to earn a customer's business. During his auto sales career, Scott applied these principles to help build his success as a car salesman, ultimately leading him to owning his own dealership, where he has built a culture that delivers a "worry-free" car-buying experience.

Scott believes everyone should enjoy the car-buying experience. But he is also aware of the fact that car dealers have earned a questionable reputation and so has made it his mission to challenge his competitors to clean up their act. He believes this can happen only through the education of consumers to help them identify and do business with those car dealers who are straightforward, ethical and honest .

Scott is married to Jennifer, is the father of five children, and a grandpa to six, soon to be seven. As a lifelong resident of Casa Grande, Az., he feels a special responsibility to give back to his community, giving his time as a Pro Tem Justice of the Peace for Pinal County, serving as president of his local high school board, and participating as an active member of Christ Life Church. As a pilot, Scott has found a special purpose in making his plane available for Angel Flights to those who are seriously ill. Scott is inspired each time by those who continue to battle against their illnesses with optimism and bravery.

Scott hopes that readers of this chapter will become better informed and that the information here will give them new insight into the car-buying process so that they are able to buy the right car, at the right price and at the right place.